BE A MENSCH

ELISA UDASKIN

BE A MENSCH

UNLEASH YOUR POWER
TO BE KIND AND HELP OTHERS

Published by Caring Organizer, LLC, Morristown, New Jersey
www.caringorganizer.com

Edited and designed by Girl Friday Productions
www.girlfridayproductions.com

Cover design: Alex Robbins
Project management: Katherine Richards
Editorial management: Tiffany Taing
Editorial: Patrick Price, Ramona Gault, Nanette Bendyna-Schuman

ISBN (paperback): 978-1-7356346-0-9
ISBN (ebook): 978-1-7356346-1-6

Library of Congress Control Number: 2020917117

For Mom, Auntie Nina, and Bubbie Regina, my three matriarchs
For my dad
All of whom shaped me into who I am today

CONTENTS

INTRODUCTION

So, first things first. What in the world is a *mensch*?

Transliterated in English as "mensch" or "mentsch," it is a word with Yiddish origins, meaning an honorable, decent person; a genuinely good person; an authentic person; a person who helps you when you need help.

mensch
/men(t)SCH/
n. a person of integrity or honor

You don't have to be Jewish to be a mensch. You can practice any religion and come from any culture and be a mensch. It isn't gender-specific, so you can identify however you do and be a mensch. It is bipartisan, so you can identify with any political party and still be a mensch.

Pretty cool.

I'd guess most people reading this book are already doing mensch-like things, yet as the title suggests, I will show you how to be an *even better* mensch in your daily life. We certainly don't want to be considered a *putz* or a *schmuck.*

putz
/putz/
n. a jerk, or a fool

schmuck
/sh-MUCK/
n. an obnoxious, contemptible, or detestable person; an idiot; a dickhead

Both words, putz and schmuck, literally mean a penis in Yiddish, but people typically use these words to call someone a jerk, not (usually) calling them directly a penis.

We all have moments when we say something we regret, overreact, and, yeah, act like a putz to someone, but overall, it's not our modus operandi. Most of us have good intentions. But what good are they if we don't get off our *tuches* and actually do something? Sitting there thinking, *I feel so bad for her that her father just died*, instead of, maybe, sending her a text? Would that be so hard to do? Actually, yes. It may well be hard and uncomfortable. I am going to explore that later in the book.

tuches
/tu-CH-ess/
n. a butt

We have so much potential to impact others in a positive way. There are literally tons of moments every day where we can make a difference. But if we aren't watching out for them, they are easily missed.

MY MOM, MY *BUBBIE,* AND ME

For me, it all started with my mom. She would talk to anyone, anywhere—at the grocery store, walking down the street, at the park. And as kids, my brothers and I would always get so embarrassed. We cringed whenever our mom stopped to talk to random strangers. At the supermarket she would offer to help someone put their groceries in their car if they looked like they needed help. (OK, truth be told, she asked one of us to do it while she chatted up the person.)

We had a joke in our family: "Who is Mom inviting over for dinner tonight? Oh, that lady she just met at the supermarket."

And it didn't stop there. She had us calling elderly relatives when they were ill to see how they were feeling. She'd take us to pay respects when someone passed away. And when we got our driver's licenses, we'd be asked to drop off food for friends of our parents who were ill. The list goes on and on. *Oy vey!*

> **oy vey**
> /OY-vay/
> *interjection.* exclamation of dismay, grief,
> or exasperation. The phrase *oy vey iz mir*
> means "oh, woe is me". *Oy gevalt!* Is like *oy
> vey,* but expresses fear, shock or amazement.

We always said, "Mom, really? Do I *have* to? I don't know them." Or simply, "I don't want to." Here's a situation between my mom and my brother Jamie. It's important to note that this took place while my brother was already an adult.

MOM: Rosy's sister-in-law in England passed away.
JAMIE: Sorry to hear that, Mom.
MOM: Rosy is very upset.
JAMIE: Mom, that's sad.

MOM: It would be very nice if you would call Rosy to offer your condolences.

JAMIE: But, Mom, I haven't seen your friend Rosy in a long time, and I have never met her sister-in-law in England. I don't want to call her. It will be too weird.

MOM: Jamie, you know when you were little, Rosy was always so good to you. She *always* brought you cookies from the bakery when she came over. *Always*. And remember a few years ago when I had that fall and broke my wrist? She made me her Indian food and brought it over. Warm. Now, *that's* a special person.

JAMIE: OK, Mom. I'll call Rosy.

You see, these were uncomfortable situations for us, but my mom didn't take no for an answer. She had (and continues to have) really high expectations of us in regard to helping others as she did. As a result, we eventually became more comfortable in these situations and saw the direct response we got from a great-aunt whose eyes lit up when she saw one of us at the door with a tray of food, or the smile on one of her friend's faces when we paid a sympathy call.

A common refrain in our house was Mom saying to Dad (in a really loud voice from a different part of the house), "Stanley, I need you to drive this soup over to so-and-so's house!" And my dad never said no. Sure, he would conveniently forget or "not hear" when my mom would ask him to unload the dishwasher, but when she would ask him to do something helpful for someone else, he always heard and did it right away. Literally, always.

Observing these simple, everyday acts of kindness by my mom (and dad), and her willingness to put herself out there, regardless of being uncomfortable or triggering others' uncomfortableness, made a big impact on me and helped to shape my life. But let's take a step back. How did my mom become who she is? The answer stems from my mom's family growing up. You see, my grandparents were Holocaust survivors, which really defined how my mom and aunt were raised, and in turn how they raised their own families.

bubbie
/bu-BEE/
n. grandmother
Other spellings include *bubbe* and *boobie.*
Some people shorten it to bubs.

zaida
/ZAY-d-AH/
n. grandfather
Other spellings include *zayde* (ZAY-DEE).

Growing up, I heard firsthand stories from my *bubbie* and *zaida* of the horrors and atrocities they experienced during the Holocaust. First, of the ghettos in their *shtetls* in Poland, then the stories of the many family members who were murdered at the hands of the Nazis and the inhumane conditions they endured in the multiple work camps and concentration camps where they were imprisoned. My zaida's four children and first wife were murdered, along with much of his extended family. Of my bubbie's six siblings, she and her two younger sisters were the only survivors. Her parents and older siblings and their children were all murdered.

shtetl
/sh-TE-TIL/
n. small village

After being liberated from the concentration camps, my grandparents met each other. My zaida was close to twenty years older than my bubbie when they married in Prague, then made their way to Germany to be with surviving family members. There they started to rebuild their life, and my mom and aunt were born. They moved to Israel for five years, but when my aunt became too ill from her asthma due to the climate, they moved back to Germany, and eventually immigrated to Canada to join my grandparents' surviving siblings, who had immigrated before them.

On the ship, they traveled with another small family who had a girl around my mom's and aunt's ages. The girl told them that they all needed to choose English names for when they came to Canada. My mom, whose name was Leeba (meaning love), chose Linda. And my aunt, whose name was Nacha (from *naches* meaning pride), chose Nina. And so ten-year-old Linda and her eight-year-old sister, Nina, arrived in the port of Halifax, Canada, in 1956. To this day, they still call each other by their Yiddish names.

They had nothing when they arrived. They didn't speak English. In fact, English was my mom and aunt's fourth language after German, Hebrew, and Yiddish. They lived in small quarters, all four of them cramped into two rooms of living space on one floor of a house. Money was scarce. My bubbie worked as a seamstress in a factory while taking in additional work on the side. My zaida was a shoemaker and opened his own shoe repair store. Eventually, through hard work and determination, they bought their own home, where they lived for many years.

What defined me the most regarding these family stories was observing and experiencing how they chose to lead their lives after the Holocaust. One might imagine, after so much being stolen from my mother's family, that they would be bitter, feeling like the world was against them. It was the opposite. Kindness to others was the central tenet in their family. Theirs was a house filled with love and gatherings of family and friends.

I was fortunate to have my bubbie in my life well into my thirties. She was always kind to my friends when she met them, but also to people whom she didn't know personally while we were out. She always had a friendly smile and something kind to say. And so, I in turn was raised in a family that demonstrated the values of kindness and optimism every day.

The biggest lesson I learned is that despite what we experience in our lives, there is always the choice to make your path one of kindness.

ABOUT THIS BOOK

This book is about relationships—how we interact with people, how we "show up." It applies to people who are close to us and people we encounter (yes, even strangers). While Yiddish is used throughout this book for its richness, humor, and forthrightness, this book is for everyone: Jewish, not Jewish, atheist, agnostic. It makes no difference who you are or where you come from. The only necessary ingredients to enjoy this book are an open mindset, someone who relishes the opportunity to grow as a person and strengthen relationships, and a sense of humor.

The concept of a mensch—as a way of talking about how we interact in the world and relate to one another in a social context—is a universal one. Being a mensch is about being a good person. It is a guidepost for living that is rich in tradition and history, but also has human truths that are common to all of us. My hope is that this book helps you access your inner mensch. Sometimes in the busyness of daily life, we silence this voice and forget that it is a part of us. But it is there. It is always there.

What this all comes down to is that it's a choice. YOUR choice. To stand back on the sidelines because you are uncomfortable, or to muster up your courage, reach out, and be kind.

Lo mir gain vaiter! Now, let's get on with it!

CHAPTER ONE

So, What's with All the Yiddish?

I grew up with Yiddish spoken around me. Not directly *to me* (God forbid the *kinde* understand all the secrets and things our parents and grandparents didn't want us to hear), but as typically happens in families where the parents speak a language with each other, the kids pick up the important stuff.

kinde
/KIN-de/
n. children

Yeah, I knew that *shayna maidele* was a pretty girl, and *nosh* was a treat. But the phrases I loved the best and that stuck with me were ones like *"Gei kachen offen yam,"* which translates literally to "Go sh*t in the ocean." This one was often said between my parents when they were disagreeing, but in a fun kind of way to tease each other.

MOM: Stanley, you didn't set the table the *right* way.
It's Shabbos!

DAD: OK, Linda.

MOM: The napkin needs to be folded *this* way with
the design side up and the fold on the *left* side,
not the right side. How many times do I need to
tell you? How many years have we been married?
How many times have you seen me do this? Why
do I have to tell you over and over again?

DAD: Linda, *gei kachen offen yam.*

Then my dad resets the table the *right* way. There is *"sha-lom ba-bayet"* (peace in the home) once again.

Another common phrase in our house when we were kids
was *"Losen gein!"* which means "Leave them alone!" It would
be used like this:

*(Dad is chasing us around the house, tickling us,
taunting us with a dead bug or spider, or giving one of
us his signature "the claw.")*

KID: Mom, make Dad stop!

MOM: Stanley, for God's sake, *losen gein!*

A quick pause for anyone not familiar with Yiddish.

Yiddish arose one thousand years ago from Middle High
German and spread throughout the ghettos of central and
eastern Europe, borrowing words from the countries in which
the Jews lived. Yiddish was one of the primary languages of
the Jews of eastern Europe prior to World War II. It is a fusion
language, written using the Hebrew alphabet, and featuring
acquired elements of Hebrew, Aramaic, Slavic, and Latin/
Romance languages.

If you didn't grow up hearing Yiddish, you may be asking yourself, "What does this Yiddish thing have to do with me?" I would say, it has *lots* to do with you. You'll soon see why, trust me. You may not speak the language or even understand it if someone told you a joke all in Yiddish, but you know it. You may not even realize how many Yiddish words you already know. Yiddish has become part of the English vernacular. Perhaps you think you are using a slang word when you say, "I *shlepped* those heavy grocery bags up two flights of stairs." Or did you know that bagel is a Yiddish word? The ubiquitous bagel originated in the Jewish communities of Poland.

shlep
/shlep/
v. to carry

How do you know and use these Yiddish words? The reason is partly because we've heard them spoken in really funny, exaggerated TV shows and movies where they make such an impact within the context of the show that you can't forget them. When you think back to a favorite scene or quote, you replay it the way it was said—using the Yiddish words and all. There's such richness, sarcasm, humor, and directness in some of these words that once you've heard them, you can only express yourself in a similar situation using that Yiddish word.

Yiddish is perfect for humorous, sarcastic, and direct ways of talking to someone in uncomfortable, awkward, and, yes, even happy occasions. Classic TV comedies where you would have heard lots of Yiddish interwoven and spoken include *Seinfeld*, *Curb Your Enthusiasm*, and *Transparent*. On *Saturday Night Live*, Mike Myers's classic character Linda Richman always got *verklempt*. In a scene from the comedic movie *Spaceballs*, Mel Brooks used the word *bubkes* ("The ring is bubkes. I found it in a Cracker Jack box.").

verklempt
/ver-klempt/
adj. feeling overwhelmed with a myriad of emotions; choked up with emotion

bubkes
/BUP-kiss/
n. nothing; trivial, worthless, useless; a ridiculously small amount

If you grew up in a Jewish household, or you are not Jewish but had friends when you were growing up who were, you probably are familiar with a lot of Yiddish terms. You may not even realize they are Yiddish when you use them as part of your regular vernacular, such as "Oh my God, it's so hot out, I'm *shvitzing*." Or, "Let's go grab a little *nosh*."

shvitz
/shv-itz/
v. to sweat

But you don't have to be Jewish, or speak Yiddish, to get the intent of these words and phrases. Yiddish is such a descriptive language that sometimes the sound of the word or expression alone can telegraph what it means.

I've grown from not noticing Yiddish or thinking about it much as a child, as it was just around me, to really loving and embracing it. There are so many words and expressions that I can only find in Yiddish to make my point. It's brazen, descriptive, honest, and direct. And it's also hilarious and gutsy. That's probably why I love *Seinfeld* and *Curb*

Your Enthusiasm so much. They're laugh-out-loud funny. The characters do the craziest *chutzpah* things that make me cringe—yet things I agree they should be doing: speaking out, being forthright, calling a spade a spade, rather than keeping their mouths shut.

chutzpah
/CHUTZ-pah/
n. gall, nerve

I identify so much with Midge, the lead character in *The Marvelous Mrs. Maisel*. She very much encapsulates the qualities of brazenness, directness, and authenticity. She's my perfect counterpart, my doppelgänger.

Yiddish gives me permission to try to overcome my inhibitions when I'm frustrated, angry, or astounded, or when I'm overcome with happiness. There's always a Yiddish expression to use that's perfect for the situation.

WHAT DO YOU MEAN I'M JUST LIKE MY MOM?

Like most teenagers and their moms, we had a rocky relationship, fighting and yelling at each other all the time growing up. My mom says that I gave her a hard time from the age of eleven until twenty. (I've always been an overachiever, so I pushed the boundaries beyond the standard teenage years.) You may think, *Oh, she couldn't have been that bad. It's normal for teenagers to push the boundaries with their parents.* Well, here's a little snippet of what an "angel" I was at fourteen, taken from a story my aunt loves to share when I *kvetch* about my own teenagers. At the time my family lived in Ottawa, while my aunt resided in Toronto.

kvetch

/k-ve-tch/

v. to complain

n. someone who complains a lot

MOM: Nacha, I can't take it anymore. Elisa is being
a total pain in the *tuches*. She argues with me all
the time and never listens. Plus she always has to
have her own way.

AUNTIE NINA: Leeba, it can't be so bad. Send her
to me.

And so my parents put me on a bus for the five-hour drive
from Ottawa to Toronto. My Uncle Jack picked me up at the
bus station downtown and took me back to their home in
Thornhill, where I spent a few hours playing with my younger
cousins, whom I adore.

Unbeknownst to me, since I naively thought I was having a
great time (and isn't that what really mattered?), my aunt called
Mom the next morning.

AUNTIE NINA: Leeba, you were right. I'm sending
her back to you.

According to Auntie Nina, this is what happened.

As soon as I came into her house and delivered hugs and
kisses, I gave my aunt a list I'd written on the bus trip of all
the places I wanted her and my uncle to take me that we didn't
have in Ottawa. (I've always been a list person.) I had money
to spend from my jobs as a cashier at our local IGA grocery
store, a babysitter, and a math tutor. So I thought this was a
reasonable request. After all, I wasn't asking them to *buy* me
things—just drive me.

My aunt was working full-time as a teacher, had three little boys, and also did as much as she could for my grandparents, as my zaida had a stroke and was in the hospital. But did any of this matter to me? Nope. I expected my aunt and uncle to drive me to all these places—including candy, clothing, and bead-supply stores—which by the way ranged from forty minutes to an hour from their home. My aunt said I was relentless in nagging her to take me, and ergo the call back to her sister to send me home! As a side note, my aunt did not actually send me home right away. I think she felt bad for my mom and wanted her to get a real break from me.

And, of course, my uncle drove me to every single place on my list.

Part of the frustration I had with my mom as a teenager was all the expectations she had of me. Even if they were the "right thing to do," I always pushed back, probably without even listening and giving her a chance that maybe she had a good idea. And she was relentless. (At least I come by it honestly.)

I was embarrassed all the time by how she would talk to anyone, anywhere. I would stand back listening to her talk to a stranger in line at the store. And when I say talk to a stranger, I don't mean little small talk. My mom had the ability to form a connection with people immediately and get them to open up, even with only five minutes in a queue. It was especially embarrassing when she would bring me into it. "Oh, your daughter is having trouble at school? My daughter over here is so good at math. You know, she tutors kids. Do you want our home number so you can call her?" How mortifying. Looking back, the truth is that my mom got me all my tutoring students. She was really good at it.

I think everyone's biggest fear is that they will turn into their parents. You'll hear people say this, but I think when they say it, they are conjuring up all the annoying things they think about their parents. They aren't pausing to think about all the amazing things about their parents as well.

When I was in my early twenties, a childhood friend made the comment to me, "You're just like your mom." I was aghast. How could she say that? It was when my friend Wendy, whom I grew up with and who knew my family well, was visiting me at university for the weekend. We were out partying on a Saturday night and I recognized a guy across the street who was two years older than we were in high school. And a popular guy at that. Pointing at him, I shouted, "Hey, that's Anthony from high school!" Wendy cringed in embarrassment, and it was then she said, "You're just like your mom."

It was funny, because that was a turning point for me. I decided that what I did wasn't so bad. Did I hurt anyone? Kill someone? No. I was just being enthusiastically friendly. And that was me.

Just like my mom.

I realized that, yes, I had morphed into my mom. And I embraced it with everything I had. In fact, at my wedding speech, I told our 319 guests that when people tell me that I'm just like my mom, I consider it the biggest compliment in the world.

And it didn't stop there. As I grew older, I became more and more like her. My mom really is the quintessential matchmaker. I believe that the character of Yente the matchmaker in *Fiddler on the Roof* was inspired by my mom. Yes, I realize that the musical *Fiddler on the Roof* debuted on Broadway in 1964, when my mom was just a teenager, but work with me on this. With her network of friends, acquaintances, and, yes, people she doesn't know personally but may have "heard of," my mom always had an eye and ear open to make a match.

People would call her and say:

"Linda, I have a niece. She's twenty-seven, lives in Toronto, and has a MASTER'S degree. Do you have someone for her?"

"Linda, my son is forty. He's divorced. It didn't work out. I really want him to meet a nice good woman. Age can be between twenty-five and thirty. Do you have someone for him?"

And then the phone call chains would begin. She always started with Auntie Nina. They would discuss the person whom they were asked to find a match for, then discuss their parents. Would they be good in-laws? So-so in-laws? And then the ball would get rolling from there.

If you can believe it, I myself have TWO successful matches under my belt. Yes, I can take credit for two friends' matches, marriages, and five kids coming from those matches. Like my mom, I also have many matches that didn't result in marriage, but you always have to try. Right?

A MENSCH OR A NUDNIK?

Along the way, I know that people have felt that I'm "too much," "too pushy," a *nudnik.* They were probably right. I am grateful for their feedback (Isn't that the appropriate thing for me to say?), but sometimes I don't understand why I come across as pushy. I'm just trying to help.

nudnik
/NOOD-nick/
n. a pest

Is offering *five* times to take over chicken soup to my neighbor who texted me she has a cold really that offensive and pushy, when she says no to the first four? I know she feels better after finally accepting the soup. Maybe she didn't want to put me out? Of course she didn't. But it was my pleasure.

I've even booked a flight to my good friend's mother's funeral, only to have her text me in a panic to please not come. She was too overwhelmed and didn't want me to spend the money on the trip. Plus she didn't think she'd have time to spend with me and it all just stressed her out.

The old me would have gone anyway. The new me listened to her and, yes, got upset. I literally then googled "what to do when your friend is grieving and they don't want your help" and found excellent articles. The key takeaway for me in these articles was that it wasn't about me, but about my friend. It was about what *she* needed, not what *I* needed.

I canceled the flight and sat at home. I took a break from texting her for two days, as I knew she felt bad about telling me not to come and I didn't want to add more stress. The morning of the funeral, I was surprised to receive a call from her. We talked about her mom and cried together. You see, she needed me, but on her terms, not mine.

For another friend, whose father passed away suddenly, my dropping everything and flying in for his funeral was what she needed. With time, I learned better how to assess and act in situations according to what the person needed, not what I needed, which was to be needed.

I've been told by people that I'm "loyal" and "they can always count on me." The best compliment I've received was when a neighbor told me that after they suddenly lost a loved one, the only thing her kids would eat that day was my home-made chicken soup. Trial and error.

THAT LITTLE VOICE IN YOUR KEPPY

keppy
/ke-PEE/
n. head

Who *isn't* afraid of what other people think of you? Of what you do, or if you, God forbid, say the "wrong" thing? That little voice in our head says, *Don't do it, it's not your place.* Or, *What if she gets mad at me?* I've been in situations where a friend was going through a difficult time and other mutual friends would say, "No, we shouldn't bother them." Even if we all wanted to support this person. Sometimes I would listen to the group and not do anything, because I didn't want to do the "wrong thing." And guess what? I always felt terrible that I didn't do anything.

Or when you hear about someone you know who is ill, or has recently passed away, and you evaluate the status of your relationship to decide what to do. *Well, she's a good friend, a really good friend. She'll want me to come over right away.* Or, *He's only a neighbor. They will have other people bringing them food. I don't want to intrude.*

I still have that little voice in my head when I have the immediate reaction to step up and help someone. But I now do my best to shoo it away and act on my first inclination—both for people I know when they are going through a difficult time, and for people I don't know. I try my best to read the situation and act accordingly, be kind, offer help, but not be too pushy. (I said I *try*—not that I always back off.) I am always met with gratitude and it is so worth overcoming my discomfort or worry that I'll embarrass my family or friends with my actions.

I've come to realize that it's important to know that you really can't go wrong. If your intentions are in the right place, you'll find the best way to reach out. So, the next time your first reaction is to reach out, try to ignore that little voice in your *keppy*. Go with your gut and be brave.

CHAPTER TWO

You're Already a Mensch (or at Least You Thought You Were)

You may be thinking:

> *I help my parents all the time.*
> *I take care of my family.*
> *I'm a good friend. My friends know I'm there for them when they need anything.*
> *I donate to causes.*
> *I give blood.*
> *I volunteer in my community.*
> *Hey, I'm already a mensch, so why should I be reading this book?*
> *I'm already giving so much of myself to others. Didn't you see the above? I only have limited time and energy for this. I'm busy. I have so much on my plate.*

Mazel tov! I agree, you are a mensch. You are a *gutte neshama.*

gutte neshama
/gu-tt-eh/
adj. good

/ne-SHA-mah/
n. a soul

Happy now? But this is exactly the point. You have the wonderful traits and talents that you are sharing and bestowing upon people already. So why not get over yourself and any hesitations or inhibitions you may have, to help and be kind in an even bigger way? You're at the tipping point of making an even greater impact with your mensch-like actions. Why stop here?

You may think you are already doing enough nice things for people, and you don't really have the energy, time, or capacity to do more. If you don't mind, I would beg to differ.

It's like when we have our first child. We love that baby so much and can't believe how we feel. Then we are pregnant with our second child and worry, *How in the world will I love this new baby as much as my first?*

Or, *I have enough friends. I don't have time for any new ones.*

Then your second child arrives and you can't believe how much you love him/her. Or you join a new book club and meet this wonderful woman whom you become friends with, or you move to a new neighborhood and all of sudden you really, really like your new neighbor, and find yourself looking forward to seeing her often.

Voilà! Your heart *does* expand to bring in more people to love—whether it's your new baby or a new friend.

The amazing thing with these two circumstances is that our hearts actually expand. It's a crazy thing that we aren't even cognizant of when it happens. It just does. And our love broadens to include new babies and new friends, all of whom enrich our lives and give us great happiness.

It's the same thing with your capacity to be kinder and to give more of yourself to others.

So, the big question is *why* should we strive to do more to help others? Even people outside our immediate circle?

The simple reason is because we can.

No matter who we are, what we have, what we don't have— we literally ALL have something to give. My bubbie used to tell us grandchildren the story of when she was in the concentration camp during the war and how she shared a potato with another girl who was starving like she was. The potato had rotten bits in it, but she would try to cut those away and share what little she had with others in need.

I remember when I was a teenager growing up in Ottawa, my brothers and I would take skiing lessons every Sunday. I did love skiing, though I was not so good at it. But what I liked most was getting poutine—an iconic Canadian *nosh* consisting of fries, cheese curds, and gravy—in the chalet during our lunch break. (It may sound gross, but believe me, it's delicious!) Around grade ten, I stopped taking those Sunday skiing lessons and skied infrequently after that.

Then on a beautiful winter day in grade twelve I made plans to go skiing with my friends. I looked in the garage where we kept our ski equipment and couldn't find mine anywhere.

ME: Mom, I can't find my ski equipment. Where is it?
MOM: Oh, I gave it away to our cleaning lady.
ME: What? I paid for most of it myself with my babysitting and grocery store job money. How could you do that?

MOM: Well, when Kasia and I were having lunch a couple months ago when she came to clean the house, we were talking about her kids. She mentioned that her daughter wanted to ski, but that the ski rentals were too expensive. So, of course, I gave them to her.

ME: But, Mom, you didn't even ask me. How did you know that I wouldn't want to use them again?

MOM: They've been sitting in the garage for over a year. You weren't using them. Someone else needed them. Done. End of conversation.

I wish I could say my mom stopped doing this after she saw how upset I was about losing my ski equipment. But no. My brothers and I had to learn that if we really wanted to keep something, we needed to keep using it. Otherwise, Mom would quickly find someone else who could, in her words, "use it more."

KINDNESS TRANSCENDS CULTURES, RELIGIONS, AND POLITICAL BELIEFS

Everyone can be kind and help others. Your background, culture, religion, socioeconomic status, and political leanings don't matter. We can all embrace it. In Yiddish, the word *rachmones* means compassion.

rachmones
/rach-MO-ness/
n. compassion

Guess what? There's a word in *every* language for compassion.

FRENCH: *la compassion*
SPANISH: *compasión*
ITALIAN: *la compassione*

You get the picture. People all over the world recognize and practice the concept. It's free to use and express. What a bargain with just one little word.

If we dig a little deeper, there are many benefits when we put ourselves out there, are kind, and help others. And this comes from experts—doctors no less—so we have to listen (or at least that is what my bubbie always thought).

Helping Others Boosts Our Happiness

Remember the *Friends* episode where Phoebe is in a quandary as she volunteers because she wonders aloud if she is being selfish when she does something nice for someone else because it actually makes *her* feel good? In the UK, researchers found that being kind could boost happiness in as little as three days.[1] The study assigned people to three groups: the first group had to do an act of kindness each day; the second group tried a new activity; and the third group did nothing. The groups who were kind and did novel things saw a significant boost in happiness.

"Why does this happen?" you may ask. Studies have shown that putting the well-being of others before our own—*without expecting anything in return*—stimulates the reward centers of the brain. These feel-good chemicals, such as serotonin, flood our system, producing a sort of "helper's high." Kindness also

---

1. "Acts of Kindness and Acts of Novelty Affect Life Satisfaction." Kathryn E. Buchanan and Anat Bardi, *The Journal of Social Psychology*, Volume 150, 2010, Issue 3, pp. 235–37.

releases the so-called love hormone, oxytocin, which raises self-esteem and makes us more positive.

I love the term "helper's high." It is so true. Imagine how you feel when you're about to eat a beautiful slice of chocolate cake. You're on a "high" of delight as you anticipate that first bite. But unlike with that beautiful slice of chocolate cake (or maybe a couple of slices if you are me), when you help someone, you don't feel a bit sluggish and full afterward. After you help someone, you just feel, well, happy. And it's a lot fewer calories.

Kindness Makes Our Relationships Even Better

There are always ups and downs in our relationships. Friends and family can boost you and make you happy; they can also piss you off and drive you *meshugenah*.

> **meshugenah**
> /me-SHOO-ge-nah/
> *adj.* crazy, insane

Doesn't it feel good when someone does something really nice for you? Or you have a phone conversation and when you hang up you're on a high? It was a real feel-good conversation. Perhaps you unloaded something that was bothering you, and your friend listened and was understanding and a real mensch.

That's another thing that kindness can do. And it's so simple. Just everyday conversations or interactions with people in our lives can make you and them happier plus strengthen your relationship.

We Have a Better Chance of Raising
Our Kids to Be Mensches

Our kids observe us all the time—even if we don't realize it. They mimic our behavior. So, if we act like a schmuck, guess what? Yeah, you know the answer. Do you remember the first time you heard your toddler, who could barely string a full comprehensible sentence together, say to someone outside your house, "That's sh*t" or "f*ck"? How did they pick up these words to add to their nascent and growing vocabulary? I think you know the answer to that one too.

If we do nice things for other people—even strangers in the supermarket—our kids will watch us be kind and, cross your fingers, mimic this behavior themselves. Indulge me as I share a story.

My family and I lived in Singapore for two years while I was on an expat assignment, leading a global team. At that time my kids were ten and twelve. Our first trip out of the very modern and developed Singapore was to Cambodia.

We were in Phnom Penh, the capital of Cambodia, and dined at a pizza restaurant one night. As we were enjoying our meal, a young boy around twelve years old approached our table to sell his goods. This kid was a spunky, outgoing, and gifted salesperson. He spoke to us in his limited English, showing off his wares and encouraging us to buy from him. Charmed, we bought a couple of bracelets and some gum and he moved on to the next table.

We finished eating yet had so much food left over. We had each ordered an individual pizza, which was so big that there was a lot left untouched. I asked our server to please bring us takeout boxes and I consolidated the leftovers into two full boxes. Since we were staying in a hotel and wouldn't be bringing the food back with us, I asked my kids to go and give the rest of the pizza to the kids who were selling outside. Aghast!

MY KIDS: We can't do that! No way!

ME: Fine, no problem.

We paid our bill and I took the boxes of pizza with me. Congregated right in front of the restaurant was this same boy we'd met earlier, along with other young people selling their stuff. With my kids lagging a bit behind me, I approached the boy and offered him the two boxes of pizza. He said thank you. As we started to walk away, what we saw was amazing. Instead of scarfing it down (which most kids would do), he called over the others, and they shared the pizza. No jostling or arguing—simply sharing.

A few days later, we left Phnom Penh for a tiny village on an island off the west coast of Cambodia. As we were waiting for our ferry, we ate pizza in a restaurant. (See a theme here?) And again, we each wanted our own thing, so we ordered individual pizzas.

Afterward, Kobi, my ten-year-old son at the time, asked if we should pack up the leftovers to give to someone. I told him that was a great idea and asked what he was thinking. He motioned to the tuk-tuk drivers waiting across the street. I asked our server to pack up the pizza and then I gave it to Kobi. Staying a short distance behind him as he crossed the way, I watched him approach the tuk-tuk drivers. Kobi outstretched his arms to give them the pizza boxes, but they were confused. As they and Kobi didn't speak the same language, they used their hands to communicate. Kobi was able to convey that no, he didn't need a ride in a tuk-tuk, but he was offering them the pizza.

They looked so surprised!

They took the pizza and nodded thank you to my son. Kobi then walked back to us and we made our way to the ferry. I told him that was a very nice thing for him to do, but I didn't make a big deal out of it. Although, believe me, I was *kvelling* inside. You see, *he* felt good about what he did and that was the main thing. I wanted this type of thing to be part of his normal behavior versus something special that he would get rewarded for from us.

kvell
/k-v-ell/
v. to burst with pride

BE THE INITIATOR

Have you ever been in a situation where you hear that a parent on your kid's hockey team or other sport or extracurricular activity is seriously ill, or they have had a death in the family, and you feel terrible but don't know what to do? So, you don't do anything but feel bad.

I know I have.

Then you receive an email or a text about a meal chain or a GoFundMe that someone else organized. Voilà! Mazel tov! You now know what you can do, and you join in and help out the family. Doesn't that feel good?

Someone just needs to get the ball rolling.

mazel tov
/MA-zel tov/
phrase. congratulations

Kindness inspires more kindness. When we perform good deeds it inspires others to follow suit. Sometimes it happens immediately, as when we provide them with a simple way they can do something to support others. Or maybe it's not until later, when they do something totally unexpected because they've observed acts of kindness from you, and it kind of "gets into their blood."

My husband, Adam, is a great guy. I consider him to be a mensch. In fact, I said that in my wedding speech when talking about how I knew he was the "right one" for me as a life partner. However, in the twenty years that we've been together, I've observed that he's not quite the *initiator* all the time when it comes to helping people he doesn't know. Strangers. I typically do the volunteer stuff, and occasionally ask him to help me out with something—which he always does. (You may at this point have observed that this is similar to my parents' relationship.)

For instance, after a neighborhood block party or other party at someone else's home, if I see there are a lot of perishable leftovers that look yummy, I'll ask the host of the party if they are saving them all. If they say there's just too much, then I ask if I can pack up some of the leftovers to take to our Market Street Mission in town for the homeless to enjoy.

That's when Adam's job comes in. I ask him to help me *shlep* everything into the car, and more often than not, I've had a couple of drinks already, so I ask him to drive us (the ten minutes) to drop the food off at the local mission.

I inevitably get a sigh from him.

ADAM: Really, Elisa? They're probably not even open at this hour.
ME: You know that even if they're officially closed, all I need to do is knock on the door and they'll be happy to take the food.

Which is exactly what happens when he begrudgingly drives me over. I knock on the door, hand over the food to the person who opens it, and often give them instructions to put everything in the fridge if they aren't eating it right away. I then get back in the car and I hear this:

ADAM: So, what did they say?
ME: They said thank you for the food.
ADAM: Cool.

And just like that, he smiles and drives us home. I know he feels good about this and what we did together. He may not express it with words. But I know. I just know.

So it came as a huge surprise when one day last winter Adam came home with a bag from his favorite Big & Tall store. Inside was a new winter jacket. (Yes, I'm married to a rare Jewish giant. Or as I like to call him, "My Gentle Giant," standing six feet five.)

ME: Isn't that the same jacket you already have?
ADAM: Yes.
ME: I don't understand. Why did you buy the same
     jacket? What happened to your other one?

(Yes, it's like pulling teeth, trying to get a complete answer out of my husband that meets my standards.)

After many more questions, he told me that he was driving in town to get a coffee when he passed a homeless man who looked really cold. It was freezing outside and the man wasn't wearing a jacket. Adam pulled his car over to the side of the road, got out, and offered this man his jacket. Adam said he didn't exactly know what came over him to do that, but he did it.

I almost *plotzed!* Nothing is sexier than seeing my husband do something kind for another. Well, maybe when he surprises me by unloading the dishwasher without me *hocking him a chinik* (nagging him).

plotz

/plotz/

v. literally, to explode, to collapse, to go
crazy because you love something so much

The moral of these stories? Do kind things and people who
watch you will follow your example and do kind things themselves. They may not even realize *why* they do these mensch
things, but they do them.

KILL THEM WITH KINDNESS

My mom taught me this one for sure. And believe me, it's not
for the faint of heart. I wouldn't expect anyone to be able to do
it consistently every time someone pisses you off, but it's worth
talking about because it does work when you give it a try.

For instance, if you're having a difference of opinion with
someone, and perhaps things get heated, you are both digging
your heels in. If you stop yourself for a second, put your "empathy hat" on, and try to think of where that other person is coming from, there's a good chance that you will calm down, and,
in turn, they will too. Or when someone cuts you off in traffic
and royally pisses you off, you have a choice. Do you honk your
horn loudly, maybe even flip them the bird? These things could
escalate the situation. Or you can think to yourself, *Maybe they
didn't realize they just cut me off.* Or, *What if they are rushing
to the hospital?* You never know what people are dealing with.

Take a deep breath and react in a positive way. It will dif-
fuse the situation. "Kill them with kindness" almost always
works.

And if it doesn't, then here's two more words of wisdom
from my mom: walk away.

OY! HERE'S WHAT THE EXPERTS SAY

If it's guidance from an expert or a doctor, of course we'll listen (at least that is what my bubbie and mother always told me). Read along, my friends.

Being Kind Is Good for Our Mental Health

I have a lot of anxiety. And stress, and anxiety again. But who doesn't? Most people either have chronic anxiety or have anxious moments at times.

Studies have shown that acts of kindness can lower our stress levels and anxiety. A study published in 1998 in the journal *Integrative Psychological and Behavioral Science* reported study subjects who were kind had 23 percent less cortisol, the stress hormone. Another study by the University of British Columbia found highly anxious people who did at least six acts of kindness per week became less anxious after a month, and their moods and relationships improved.[2]

So all I have to do is be kind and I'll feel better? Sold!

Physical Benefits

Kindness can also help your physical body. Bye-bye dieting! Just be kind, help someone, and eat that second slice of beautiful chocolate cake.

Well, not quite. I would never say that being kind will help you with your expanding waistline, but there are plenty of proven health benefits worth mentioning. A study at the University of California, Berkeley found that 50 percent of the

---

2. https://thriveglobal.com/stories/the-power-of-kindness-2/.

participants who did kind deeds reported having more energy.[3] Being kind can even relieve pain, because being kind produces endorphins, which make you happy. According to an article in Thrive Global, "researchers at the University of the South found that performing acts of kindness can help you move past painful experiences more than selfish indulgences."

The article goes on to ask, "What's the most compelling reason to be kind? It can extend your lifespan. Kindness is how we gain and keep friends. Friends keep us happy and healthy. Without them, we are at a larger risk for heart disease. Christine Carter of UC Berkeley found that people 55+ who volunteered for at least two organizations were 44 percent less likely to die early."[4]

To sum up all this awesome research, the more acts of kindness we share with others, the better we will feel emotionally, psychologically, and physically. And here's the icing on the cake. Acts of kindness can be anonymous or visible, spontaneous or planned, and as simple as giving a compliment or opening a door for someone. Easy as pie!

NU, IF IT'S SO GOOD FOR US TO HELP OTHERS, THEN WHY DON'T WE DO IT ALL THE TIME?

> **nu?**
> /noo/
> *interjection.* So? Huh? Well?

I am no doctor, PhD, or expert of that sort, but I do have a confession to make. I love to talk to people. And by people, I mean strangers, friends, literally whoever will give me a couple

---

3. https://thriveglobal.com/stories/the-power-of-kindness-2/.
4. https://thriveglobal.com/stories/the-power-of-kindness-2/.

of minutes of their time (if it wasn't already obvious). This is what I've found out from asking people lots of questions and listening. Combined with reading and researching, common themes emerged.

No Time

People think it will take a lot of time to help someone out.

"I don't have time."

"I'm too busy."

Well, you actually *do* have the time (for heaven's sake, it only takes a couple of minutes in some instances). In fact, did you know that the busier we are, the more productive we are? This means that we are all superheroes and can accomplish so much more the more we have on our plate. So, keep your ears open, and when you hear of a friend, family member, or acquaintance in your community who is going through a tough time, reach out and send them support. It can be a quick message, a meal, or an offer to help with a ride.

You can fit it in. And it will make you feel so good too. Fitting it in means making it a priority. Trust me, it will not take up hours each day. I promise. It can be as simple as waking up and thinking, *Who needs my help today?* And then perhaps texting your friend who is going through cancer just to check in and let her know you are thinking of her. That's it. Simple.

What I've come to realize is that I don't always have to make a grand gesture to make it meaningful. For instance, if I can't figure out how to make the time for an in-person visit, I can send my friend a text to check in on them, or better yet call them and be an open ear to listen. It's the simple and small things we do for people every day that can make the biggest impact, especially when they are going through a difficult time. And the best part about it is that it doesn't need to take a lot of time to show how much you love them and care.

Procrastination

Sometimes (OK, maybe often) I get overwhelmed with how much I need to do every day. I have high expectations of myself and set giant goals. I want to do it all. And when someone I care about is going through a hard time, I want to do something *meaningful*, but often I procrastinate because I overthink things.

What should I do?

Will they think it's strange?

Maybe I'd be bothering them, so I shouldn't text right now. They must be so stressed out.

And then I decide that *tomorrow* I'll reach out or do that online memorial donation. And then tomorrow becomes the next day, then the next week, and . . . well, you get the idea.

We all procrastinate, especially when it's about something that is emotional, or when we aren't entirely sure if it's the right thing to do. This is totally normal. What's important is to follow through with it eventually, even if time has passed.

It's never too late to show your support. People will appreciate it.

What Will They Think of You?

Another reason we hesitate to reach out is that we are worried about what people will think of us—the person we reach out to, others who observe what we do, people who hear about it. Others can be so judgmental, and it comes from everywhere! I care a lot about what other people think of me. I wish I didn't so much, but what can I do? I try, though, to overcome it and press on almost all of the time.

But who really cares? What is the worst thing that can happen? More important, what is the *best* thing that can happen? Be vulnerable. Reach out. Nothing really bad will happen. Yeah, it may be awkward, even uncomfortable at times, but it's always worth giving it a shot. Don't be afraid of giving of yourself, putting yourself out there. Don't listen to those voices in your head that make you hesitate.

Ignore your kid saying, "Mom, you're embarrassing me."

Disregard the nosy busybody who says, "Who does she think she is? She's overstepping."

It's THEIR fear of what people will think. Don't let it be yours.

At least that's what I try to do. Believe me, I get this all the time from my kids and my husband. And then I overthink things and it nags at me for a long time, whereas they've moved on and don't give it another thought.

Please don't judge others when they reach out or step in, and you just want to cringe at what they are doing. Instead, turn it on its head and admire how brave they are. We all react differently in situations. Most of us have good intentions. Let's celebrate that.

It's Not Your Place

Now this one in my opinion is ridiculous. Of course it's your place to be kind and supportive. However, I think what's valid in this thought is WHAT you do, not THAT you do something. If you feel that there are other people closer to someone you want to support who are their more "hands-on" or "go-to" person, then do something that's not as intrusive but that shows you care. We'll talk more later about things you can still do in these types of situations.

You Don't Want to Bother Them

Of course you don't! Why in the world would you want to bother someone—especially if they are going through a difficult time? But you know what is worse for that person than someone "bothering" them? NO ONE reaching out to them!

I've heard it countless times when someone has been ill or a family member passed away and others are too timid to reach out and express support. People have been hurt and disappointed by the "silence." They say:

> "Now I really know who my friends are."

> "Now I really know who I can count on."

> "I was surprised that the people I thought I could count on weren't there. But then people who I didn't expect to reach out were so kind."

I bet you that the people who let others down didn't do it on purpose. I'm sure they thought of their friend, but didn't know what to do, then worried that too much time had passed when they didn't do anything so it was too late. The list goes on. Or maybe they just aren't the type of person who does things for others.

It could be. I hope not. But it could be. What happens is, it irrevocably changes their relationship. I've literally heard this story a million times.

You Live in a Bubble

Here's the reality. We live in a very insular world. Our circle is small and the people and things we typically pay attention to are the people who are right in front of us. As our lives become busier and busier, our lens becomes even smaller.

Part of being a mensch is understanding that our circle should go well beyond the people under our roof. Yes, they are our primary focus, but we need to make the effort to train our brain to see outside of our own bubble. Expand our circle and the number of people whom we share our awesome kindness with.

You Fear Rejection

Rejection sucks. You muster up your courage and offer to bring dinner to a friend or acquaintance, or you send them a text and they don't want the dinner, or they may not even answer your text. And you feel terrible.

"Did I do something wrong to upset them?"

"Why won't they let me bring over dinner?"

"Why wouldn't she text me back? It's been three days already. I keep checking my phone every five minutes."

If people aren't ready to receive or accept your help when you offer it, you have to try as hard as you can to not take it personally. Try to remember that THEY are the ones going through the rough time. Not you. Again, it's about them, not you. Keep repeating this in your head, or perhaps out loud if that helps. (That's what I do—I'm an external processor after all.)

When they are ready, they will get back to you. And may even take you up on making your famous lasagna for them. Don't let this dissuade you completely. Take their cues. Pull back for the time being. Don't be offended.

And don't give up. You can still do something to support them down the line when they are more ready to accept your kind offer of support.

But You Haven't Been in Touch in Years

This in fact is one of the best reasons why you SHOULD reach out to someone who you've heard has lost a loved one or is ill. Because it is even more special when we reconnect with people we were fond of but whom we've lost touch with over the years, and especially when they reach out to show they care. It brings back warm memories of when we were closer, and that can make us feel better during really difficult times.

We all have something to give. And there are so many ways to show kindness and support when someone we know could use an extra little bit of love. One of the best ways I've found to show my love and support is through the universal power of food—cooking for someone or sending them a little treat to brighten their day.

CHAPTER THREE

Ess, Mein Kinde, Ess

ess
/ess/
v. to eat

mein kinde
/mine KIN-de/
n. my children

THE ALMIGHTY POWER OF
HOMEMADE CHICKEN SOUP

When I think about what meal or food brings back memories, there is no question that it's my bubbie's chicken soup. Bubbie Regina would make her soup for us every Friday night for Shabbat and holidays, with her homemade *kreplach* or matzoh balls. And, of course, she always made her soup when one of her daughters, sons-in-law, or grandchildren was sick. No *kreplach* or matzoh balls when we were sick, just the *yo'ach*.

kreplach
/krep-lach/
n. a dumpling

yo'ach
/YO-ach/
n. broth

No matter what the illness—a common cold, the flu, or even chicken pox—the soup would be delivered to our house, and our mom would set out a bowl for us.

MOM: Ess, ess.
KID: Mom, but I'm not hungry.
MOM: It doesn't matter. Eat the soup. It will make you feel better.
KID: But, Mom, I don't want to. I'm not hungry.
MOM: Do you know how much work it took your bubbie to make it?

We would slurp up the soup.

And miraculously, we would feel better.

After my bubbie passed away, my mom took over the chicken soup helm. If for a Shabbat dinner my mom and aunt wanted to change things up a bit—maybe a tomato lentil or vegetable soup—that was my aunt's domain. But we all knew that Auntie Nina didn't like to touch raw chicken, so it was always my mom doing the honors for the chicken soup.

I never made a chicken soup myself until my late thirties, when we moved away from Toronto to New Jersey. Why would I? There was never a reason to do it myself. It was always readily available for me when I needed it—my mom all too willing to drop it off at our house when Adam or I or one of my kids was not feeling well.

I remember the very first time we made chicken soup on our own. It was Rosh Hashanah (the Jewish New Year) in 2009. I was working at an event in New York City that day and was only going to get home in time for dinner. Of course, we were going to have guests join us for Rosh Hashanah dinner. So Adam took the helm. He called my mom and asked her for the recipe.

> ADAM: Hi, Linda. Can you please email or text me the recipe for your chicken soup?
> MOM: Recipe? What recipe? I don't have a recipe written down. It's easy to make, don't worry.
> ADAM: But I've never made it before. I think I need a recipe.
> MOM: Just clean the chicken. Put it in a pot and cover with water. Cut up carrots, celery, parsnips, onions, some parsley, and let it boil.
> ADAM: How many carrots?
> MOM: I don't know, just a few carrots. You'll know.

And the "recipe" unfolded like that.

The soup was delicious, of course. I think my mom may have stayed on the phone with Adam throughout making the soup—maybe not. But it turned out amazing and tasted just like my mom's.

The next time, I told Adam *I* would try to make the soup. What I found totally caught me off guard. I really enjoyed cleaning the raw chicken. It became a challenge for me to get it as clean as I could, removing most of the fat. And I had bought a new pair of kitchen scissors especially for this task. I know, weird, right? I'm not sure if we could consider this a fetish, but all the same, I enjoyed it.

While the chicken was boiling for an hour, I cut up all the vegetables. And I got into a rhythm. It soothed me; it comforted me. Then I added the vegetables to the pot and cooked it for a couple more hours as the aroma wafted through the house. The experience was better than meditation. It was unbelievable how this cooking ritual made me feel.

From then on, I became the chief chicken soup maker in our house. When I would serve it to our guests at Shabbat dinner or Rosh Hashanah, I would receive compliments, and that fueled me even further in my quest to become the CHIEF chicken soup maker in Morristown, New Jersey.

When someone in my house was sick, I would make chicken soup. It was time-consuming with all that cleaning the chicken and chopping the vegetables, but I loved doing it. Then I got smart. I started to double, even triple, the usual amount that I made, so that I could freeze the soup for when we needed it when someone was sick. I started to drop it off to neighbors when I heard they were ill (even with just a common cold).

When I made the soup, I felt a strong sense of purpose. Not only was I feeding our family and friends during holidays, but I was nourishing my "village" when they needed it.

True soul food. Not only for the people who consumed my soup, but for me. True magic.

Here's my bubbie's chicken soup recipe, transcribed from my mom. The measurements aren't exact, so take it with a grain of salt. The most important thing to make it delicious is to feel it in your soul as you are making the soup and let the aromas fill your house with love, comfort, and warmth (sorry to be so *schmaltzy*, but I really believe this).

schmaltzy
/SHMAL-tzee/
adj. corny

BUBBIE REGINA'S CHICKEN SOUP RECIPE

What You'll Need:

2 4-lb. (4.4 kg) chickens, cut up

2 cooking onions, peeled and quartered

6 garlic cloves, skin removed

4 stalks celery, trimmed and cut into sticks

5 large carrots, peeled and cut into sticks

3 large parsnips, peeled and cut into sticks

1 kohlrabi, peeled and cut into cubes (may omit if you cannot find in the store)

1 bunch parsley

2 tsp. salt

Instructions:

1. Remove excess fat from the chicken pieces. Place in a large pot and add water to cover (about 4 inches above the chicken). Bring to a boil and skim off the scum that rises to the top. Reduce heat and simmer for 30 to 45 minutes.

2. Add onions, garlic cloves, celery, carrots, parsnips, kohlrabi, parsley, and salt. Continue to simmer for another hour.

3. Cool slightly, then use a large slotted spoon to remove chicken bones and parsley. Add more salt as desired.

Tips:

Slice off the meat from the chicken and use to make another recipe such as chicken salad or a stir-fry. (We don't want to waste anything.) Either use right away or place in a Ziploc bag with a marinade and put in the freezer.

This soup freezes very well. Let cool completely, then pour into large Ziploc bags and lay flat in freezer to stack them. Or use any other container to freeze.

Recipe can be halved if a smaller batch is desired. (But why bother? You'll want *all* this soup.)

UNLEASH YOUR INNER *BALABOOSTA*

Nu, what is this word *balaboosta*, and why are we talking about it here? It's such a strange word, no?

balaboosta
/ba-la-BOO-sta/
n. a good homemaker
Alternatively spelled *balabusta*.

The traditional definition of a *balaboosta* is a good homemaker, a woman who's in charge of her home. She cooks, she cleans, she takes care of her family. As Wikipedia puts it, "The traditional role of the balabusta also includes, besides fulfilling the household duties for the family, its spiritual bonding and helping its members hold together."[5]

When I picture a balaboosta in my head, I think immediately of my bubbie. Her homemade kreplach and chicken soup, her infamous "bubbie cake" (the most delicious chocolate strudel ever), her habit of hemming pants, sewing missing buttons on all our clothes, and organizing our closets when she visited (which I hated when I was a teenager and came home from school to see my grandmother had gone through all the stuff in my closet). In my mind, a balaboosta was a loving old woman

---

5. https://en.wikipedia.org/wiki/Balabusta; see also https://balabusta.com/.

who was solely a homemaker, not doing paid work outside the home. Her family was her life.

This shouldn't have been my view, as my bubbie had always worked all her life, but my memories of her are mostly from when she wasn't working outside the home any longer and was just taking care of us.

As a "career woman," I never ever would have wanted to be referred to as a balaboosta. I worked hard to earn my stripes in the corporate world and wanted to be perceived as a strong, assertive, kick-ass marketer and leader, not as someone who stayed home cooking and cleaning for her family. Heaven forbid.

Then something transformational happened in my outlook on my life that changed how I viewed what a balaboosta was, and I saw what an amazing compliment and honor it would be to actually be considered one myself.

While living and working in Singapore, I received coaching from my friend Dalia Feldheim, who was becoming certified to be a life coach. I was one of her first clients as she worked toward her certification. Dalia was a kick-ass marketer as well as an organizational psychologist. After a successful twenty-year career at Procter & Gamble Company and Electrolux, living and working in Israel, Russia, Switzerland, and then Singapore, she decided to make a major career shift. She became a yoga instructor and a life coach. (A few years later, she added TEDx speaker, accomplished coach, and author to her pedigree.) Dalia was someone I could really relate to as I was also yearning at that time to explore new opportunities but was scared to make a change.

Dalia led me through exercises to look at my life holistically, not only through the lens of my career and work as I was doing at that time. When we started the coaching process and she first asked me what my priorities were, I easily answered work, then family, travel, volunteering, etc. I approached my life this way. I would work really hard so that I could provide the opportunities for my family that I strove for. The focus for me started with work. Always. And believe me, I loved my work. Loved the excitement, challenges, travel, and especially the people I worked with. I just loved it.

But as I worked with Dalia, what I put down on paper regarding my holistic goals for my life surprised me. After she coached me hard and encouraged me to really be honest with myself, my number one goal was the well-being of my family, including raising my kids to be mensches—or as I further articulated it (coaches make you do that, you know), "solid contributors to society and just good people."

I also acknowledged sheepishly that I absolutely love to cook for my family and friends, to nourish them both on regular days and especially on holidays, bringing our traditions to life through food. Nothing excited me more than the challenge of making chicken soup with *lokshen* and matzoh balls for our first Rosh Hashanah in Singapore. I substituted rice noodles for the egg noodles (*lokshen*) I couldn't find. I then got crafty and when my parents visited a few months later from Toronto, I asked them to bring me some essentials. They dedicated an entire suitcase to matzoh ball mix, lokshen, and other soul foods I craved yet couldn't easily find in Singapore.

lokshen
/lok-shen/
n. noodles

This was around the time when Instagram started to become popular. I've never been an early adopter of technology. Perhaps a midstage adopter, or even a late adopter. When I finally got on the bandwagon of this Instagram trend, I needed to set up my profile. And this is what immediately popped into my head for my personal description, which I still have for my @elisaudaskin profile today, five years later:

Global Balaboosta
hockey mom, marketer, aspiring to bring
smiles around the world.

Holy sh*t, my priorities in terms of how I viewed myself had changed from the first time I had a coaching session. I needed to think about my life holistically—what I loved, what I didn't love so much, and what I wanted out of my life. I was finally being truer to myself.

I embraced the term "balaboosta" and made it my own. A kick-ass person who cares for and nurtures her family and friends . . . while also doing many *other* kick-ass things in her life, including having a career. A modern version!

And here's another amazing thing. Balaboostas exist in *every* culture—perhaps with different names, but they are the same type of person. Think of the Italian mama, the *ama de casa*. And while the technical translation is female, I would argue that any gender can be a balaboosta. It's in your soul, how you care for and take care of people.

"TAKE A TASTE OF THIS. DOESN'T MATTER IF YOU'RE FULL, JUST A TASTE."

Just like all the bubbies, grandmas, grannies, yayas, and nonnas out there, many of us nourish others and show our love through food. And when someone we know has an ill family member or a death in the family, we like to make them food, send them food, and order them food. Or even send a little nosh if it's not a full meal.

One of the best feelings I get is when I have the opportunity to bring dinner over to a friend or neighbor going through a rough time. It may help them out, but really it makes me feel good. I try to always have extra chicken soup in the freezer to warm up for someone in my family when they aren't feeling well or to drop off to a neighbor. I've even experimented with which are the best containers to store soup in the freezer, as believe me, it's no small feat. I don't want the soup to take up all the space in my freezer. What I've found to be the best is pouring the cooled-down soup into Ziploc freezer bags and then stacking them on top of one another in a nice neat space.

Things are always so busy, but I try as much as I can to keep my mind on the people in my life who are going through rough times. It keeps me in check and is a great reminder to my own little family that things are not always about us.

FOOD IS HOW WE SHOW PEOPLE WE CARE

What is a more mensch-like thing to do than to feed people who are going through a hard time? Food is a universal symbol of comfort. It draws people together and comforts them in times of need. Food is how we show people we care about them and love them. It can be comforting and healing both for the person you are cooking for and for you.

After a funeral, food typically plays a large role. While traditions in mourning vary by culture, one thing is a near guarantee—showing love and support with food is universal, whether it be sending in food for *shiva* meals (Jewish), a repast meal (Catholic), or any other religion.

Everyone talks about the food at a *shiva*.

> **shiva**
> /shi-VAH/
> *n.* the weeklong mourning ritual in Judaism honoring the dead

At a shiva, typically the immediate family mourns for seven days, receiving visitors who pay their condolences and send an abundance of food. The mourners are together a lot. They share meals, and after all this intense time together, what more is there to talk about?

The food, of course.

"The chicken from Schwartz's was so much better than the one from Goldstein's. You should tell them."

"Oy, chicken again?" Variety, people. Variety is key.

"BUT I'M NOT A BALABOOSTA—I DON'T COOK!" YOU SAY

So, you don't cook, or don't like to cook. You have a phone? A credit card?

Order from a restaurant and deliver!

Remember what we talked about earlier? Being a balaboosta doesn't mean you only cook for your family. The concept is broader than that, in my opinion. It's taking care of your "village" in any way you can.

When you don't have the time to prepare a meal yourself, or frankly you don't like to cook, don't worry—the most important thing is making the effort. Just please, for me, don't make excuses not to do anything. Order from a local restaurant and either have it delivered directly to their home or pick it up and take it over. Nowadays, it's easier than ever to order a meal to be sent to someone you care about, even if you live far away. Services like Uber Eats, Grubhub, and the like are available in most communities if you want to order and have the meal delivered directly for you.

MENSCH THINGS YOU CAN DO

Be a mensch! Here are a few helpful tips when you are sending a meal to support a family:

- Always find out if there are any specific food preferences or restrictions in the family.
- Chicken is a natural go-to for most people, so you might want to think of an alternative, as chicken every night can get boring. When people are receiving a meal every day, they really appreciate variety.
- Food represents comfort, so make the delivery personal. Including a handwritten note is a meaningful way of sending a personal message to the recipient.
- Look for things that either are easy to heat up or can be served at room temperature and require little to no effort for them to enjoy.
- Send the meal in disposable containers and include disposable plates, cutlery, and cups. Returning your favorite serving dish should not be their added worry or concern.
- Include a label or recipe card with heating instructions, if applicable. List the ingredients in case there are any allergies.
- If you are delivering the food yourself, don't overstay your welcome. The family may not be up for a long visit, so make it clear that you are just there to drop off the meal.

CHAPTER FOUR

Are You *Meshugenah*?

"Don't talk to strangers!" Hasn't this been drummed into our heads since we were little? Haven't we all said that to our own kids a million times?

We were raised to "not talk to strangers" and "keep the doors locked in the house." We watched too many movies where the hitchhiking teen was kidnapped, or the taxi driver turned out to be a serial murderer. Or my favorite (read sarcasm here) was when I babysat as a young teen and after *The Love Boat* and *Fantasy Island* were over, the local news flashed up with "It's eleven o'clock. Do you know where your children are?" This literally still haunts me to this day. When I see it's eleven o'clock and my own teenagers are out, I may panic just a little and maybe even send them a text to confirm they are OK.

However much we want to reach out, we are often very cautious or scared when it comes to approaching, let alone helping, a stranger. We feel nervous and tentative. Some people look away, look down, or even cross the street when they pass a homeless person. They hold their kids tighter to them and tell them to "walk faster."

I still remember when this message cemented in my brain. To be honest, it was totally confusing. Let me explain.

It was the mid-seventies and I was a little kid. My mom, my two little brothers, and I were driving along Finch Avenue in Toronto. Mom saw two kids around ten years old, a boy and a girl, with their thumbs up, trying to hitch a ride. Did Mom know them? No. Were they strangers? Yes.

My mom surprised us by pulling over to the side of the road. She asked me to roll down my window (we didn't have automatic windows then; you needed to crank them open). To the two kids she said, "Get in."

What happened next horrified me. Mom started laying into these two kids, admonishing them for hitchhiking, lecturing them it's not safe, and they should *never* do it again. When she caught her breath, she asked them where they wanted her to drive them.

Then she shouted to the back of the car, "Elisa, can you give these kids a couple of cookies that you have back there? Now! Not later. They must be hungry."

Well, that was confusing.

From that day on, I was afraid to hitchhike for fear that a woman would pick me up and yell at me. And once I got my license at sixteen, I would think about what happened with my mom in the car that day with the two kid hitchhikers. I always scan the road to see if someone needs help because that's what my mom did. But then I have this inner conflict about not talking to strangers, let alone picking someone up who looks like they need help.

After many years of contemplation, I have decided that there is a way to be safe *and* talk to strangers *and* help a stranger. It's about using your *sekhel*. What I mean by this is, assess the situation (quickly, I might add) to make sure it's safe to do so.

And if you don't think it's safe, you have a phone, no? Use it to call for help.

sekhel
/SEH-khul/
n. common sense, good judgment

I really don't think our parents (or most parents) intended for us to be rude or to block ourselves off completely from other people when they preached "Don't talk to strangers." They just wanted to teach us to be aware always, use our sekhel, and be safe.

Have *rachmones* (compassion). We are now so paranoid and overly cautious that we have lost some of that will to interact with people we don't know, either helping them or simply just being a mensch and smiling when we pass them by.

YOU CAN CHOOSE TO BE A MENSCH INSTEAD OF A SCHMUCK

We've all been there in some way or fashion. You are in line at the supermarket and the person in front of you is price checking as their items are being scanned, and just when you think things are going smoothly and your turn will be in a couple of minutes, the person speaks to the cashier in an exasperated voice.

CUSTOMER: $2.99? What? No. The sign said this cheese is on sale for $1.99.
CASHIER: Ma'am, the price is coming up $2.99.
CUSTOMER: I'm telling you it's $1.99. Don't you believe me?

The customer then stands back a little bit and crosses her arms. She's not budging. Then . . .

CASHIER (talking into their microphone): Price check requested at register seven.

Oy abrocht!

Oy abrocht
/oy-A-brocht/
interjection. What a catastrophe!

You were so close. But alas, not your turn. You have a million things to do after the grocery store. You're already running behind. Now you have to wait for the stock person to get to your cashier, find out the item to check, walk to the back of the store where the cheese is to check the price, then walk back to your cashier. Heaven forbid he run. No, you know he's going to walk.

And you are getting more and more impatient.

Finally the price checker is back. And he tells the cashier that the cheese is indeed $2.99, not $1.99. That sign was for the cheese next to the one that the customer was buying.

This same customer then takes more time looking through her wallet for coupons. And you are standing there behind her with only two items!

You are on the brink of losing your sh*t.

Do you huff and puff loudly, making sure that the customer in front of you and the cashier (and everyone else nearby) hear you? Do you give them the death stare? Or do you take a deep breath and realize it's probably only another five, maybe six, minutes tops out of your day and it's not such a big deal?

Now imagine you are driving and the person in front of you is SUPER slow. Cars behind you start to honk, and you wish you could hang a bumper sticker on the back of your car that reads: IT'S NOT ME! IT'S THE SLOWPOKE IN FRONT OF ME. STOP HONKING! It causes stress, that's for sure.

Yet another common situation. Sorry if this is making your blood pressure rise. It's making mine rise just remembering these situations when they happen to me (all real).

Or you are at the shopping mall, where it seems there is only one public washroom on each floor and it's far away from where you are. You first try to locate the mall's map. Finally you find it and realize that the public washroom is at the other end of the mall from where you are currently standing. OK, you can do this. You hold it in and start walking briskly, clenching your *tuches* and other body parts so that you don't *pish* yourself.

pish
/pish/
v. to pee, to urinate

Thank goodness, you finally get there. And then you see there's a long lineup. *You've got to be kidding me.* You continue to focus on holding it in, squirming as you patiently wait your turn in line. Then a young mother comes up the line saying loudly to everyone, "My daughter needs to pee really bad. Can she please go ahead of you all?"

Inevitably people will grumble. Some will think, *I'm sure that kid can hold it in for a bit longer.* Others will think, *But I've been waiting in this line for five minutes already and I'm about to lose it.*

My best advice in this type of situation is to assess your immediate need. Do you think you could hold it in for a few more minutes? If so, then why not give the kid a chance to pee first? A few extra minutes will not make an impact on your life, but for this little kid and the mom, it could be the difference between a three-minute pish or a fifteen-minute ordeal when she pishes her pants and cries uncontrollably, and her mom needs to stuff tons of toilet paper into her pants as a temporary solution till she can change the kid into dry clothes.

There are so many everyday situations that present us with a choice of how to act. Literally, every day. Most of the time in these situations, we are stressed or rushed, or the other person we encounter is stressed or rushed. And BANG! When you collide, it can be an explosive interaction or even just a yucky interaction. Or it can be a good one.

You decide. It's really up to you how you handle your reactions. Are you going to be a mensch or a schmuck?

You don't have to be perfect to be a mensch. Everyone has schmuck moments. The important thing is to be more aware of how you are reacting to situations, so you can make a choice that feels good to you.

Here's what Annie Lennox had to say about this: "Ask yourself: Have you been kind today? Was anyone kind to you? How did it feel? When that obnoxious person pushed in front of you in the supermarket queue, did you spontaneously verbally or physically head-butt them to point out their rude behavior, or did you simmer in silence, only to kick the car half an hour later? Did that make you feel better? Probably not. It can be quite a curious exercise to try to react differently in certain situations, just to see how the outcome can be affected. For example, when other people are being rude or aggressive, the most obvious reaction is to top their behavior by being even more vile in retaliation. I'm the first one to admit that sometimes it's almost impossible to prevent this kind of response. But interesting things start to happen when you decide to take charge and break this pattern of disconnectedness by applying the kindness factor. What could be a nasty situation gets defused. You make contact instead of conflict. You end up smiling instead of raging. So make kindness your daily modus operandi and change your world."[6]

Road rage. We've either been part of it or at the very least witnessed it. Don't tell me you haven't, because that's literally impossible. I have two stories of road rage where I reacted in totally different ways. In one situation I was a total putz; in the other I tried to be a mensch.

I was on my way to my exercise class at Barre3 on South Street, the main street of Morristown. South Street is notorious (keep in mind when I say notorious, I mean in my little town of Morristown, New Jersey) for being an extremely hard place to find a parking spot, if you don't want to shell out the big bucks for the paid parking lot.

As I was scanning both sides of the street for a spot, I saw one open up in front of Barre3. Yeah, I scored! I pulled up just in front of the spot and put my right-turn signal on, preparing for my awesome parallel park. As I looked in my rearview mirror to start backing into the spot, another car swooped in from behind me and took the spot.

What the heck?

I couldn't let that go, that's for sure. I put my car into park and got out with the intention of letting the other person know that he took my spot. I'm not sure if I was planning to push it all the way and ask the guy to move out so I could rightly take the spot. Honestly, I wasn't really thinking at all, just reacting.

ME: Hey, that was my spot. Didn't you see I had my
     blinker on and was waiting for the traffic to pass
     so I could back in?
GUY: Lady, whatever.
ME: Excuse me? What did you say?
GUY: Lady, just get back in your car.

---

6. *A Revolution in Kindness*, by Anita Roddick, ed. Anita Roddick Books, 2003.

At this point, the cars started to pile up behind us, as I was blocking the street with my car double-parked on the side of this very busy street (again, in Morristown, not New York City, but stressful all the same).

> ME: You are not a very nice man. Stop yelling at me.
> (I was probably yelling, not even realizing the irony of this.)

As we were yelling at each other, I saw that another passenger in his car was helping an elderly lady get out of the back seat and to the walker that she had placed on the sidewalk. *Sh*t.*

> GUY: Lady, you're crazy. Get back in your car.

At which point, I gave up and got into my car, driving away shaking, literally shaking. This guy was an asshole. Why couldn't he have just nicely said to me that he had an elderly passenger in his car, that he needed a close spot, instead of swooping in to take mine and then yelling back at me?

And why did I feel I needed to stop my car to make my point, when I could easily have circled the block looking for another spot or, yes, succumbed to parking in the paid lot just around the corner?

This encounter left me shaken all day long (and clearly, I *still* think about it, as I'm sharing it with you now). Was it really necessary for me to get myself all worked up, get this guy all worked up, and cause a scene on South Street?

A few weeks later I'm back on South Street and encounter a similar situation. (I'd been back to South Street many times in between, but let me tell you the story.) I was meeting a friend for lunch and found a sweet parking spot on the east side of South Street a few doors down from the restaurant. While I was putting my quarters in the parking meter, I heard a ruckus across the street. A man was double-parked in his pickup truck, blocking traffic and refusing to move. The cars behind him were honking furiously. He started to shout out his window, "That guy took my parking spot! I'm not moving until he moves out. That's my spot!"

People walking on both sides of the sidewalk stopped to watch. Then I remembered what had happened to me a couple of weeks before and how awful I felt about it. I noticed that there was an open parking spot on my side of the street just ahead of where I parked. I walked over, stood in the middle of the spot on the street, and shouted over to the driver in the truck, "I have a spot for you. I'll stand here to save it for you until you turn around and come park."

People standing on the sidewalk then started to talk to the driver as well, trying to calm him down. "Sir, take that spot over there where that woman is standing. It's not worth it. Other cars need to drive by."

The man in the truck started to drive. Everyone on the street, the oncoming traffic too, stopped to let him turn around, and he parked in the spot that I was holding for him.

You see, all the bystanders, including myself, agreed with him—it *was* a putz move on the part of the driver who took his spot. What was really cool was that these strangers and I worked together to find a solution and try to calm down the truck driver.

Boy, do I wish I had had someone to calm me down when I was pissed a couple weeks earlier.

The next time a situation like this arises, do your best to respond with empathy instead of frustration or anger. Deep breaths, my friends. Deep breaths.

GIVE PEOPLE THE BENEFIT OF THE DOUBT

I have spent a lot of time in airports, traveling for work when I was on a global team. And I spent lots of time in lines for security and immigration. There's nothing more frustrating than checking in with your airline, then walking over to the boarding gates line and *bam!* you see a huge line. You immediately look at your boarding pass to check the boarding time. Then look at the line ahead of you to gauge how long you think it will be to get through. Then check your boarding pass again. And so on and so on.

Has this situation ever happened to you? You're in a long line at the airport to check your ID and go through the security line when you hear someone from behind you in line frantically asking if he could please pass ahead as his flight is leaving in thirty minutes. This kind of person is almost always waving his boarding pass in the air with one hand while the other hand is dragging his carry-on luggage. And he is usually also shvitzing.

You may think to yourself, *Well, he should have left himself more time to get to the airport before his flight.* Yes, your judging hat comes on immediately. And I'm sure everyone else in the queue is thinking the same thing. Didn't we have to leave enough time to get to the airport for our flight? Why is this putz any different and why should he get any special treatment?

However, maybe you consider that he could have indeed left with enough time, but there was an accident on the way to the airport that delayed him and wasn't in his control.

Ahhhhhh. That *could* be a possibility.

Have empathy. Check your boarding pass and if it looks like you will definitely have enough time yourself, then let him ahead of you. You can even take this situation one step further. If you see that some people are hesitating to let him in, be brave (polite) and help speak up for him to the passengers in front of you to plead his case. It works every time. Yes, I've been guilty of doing just this a number of times and in different airports around the world.

Doesn't everyone have a bad day once in a while? Aren't people entitled to have a bad day? Aren't you?

You never know what people are dealing with when they "show up" in a negative way and are inconsiderate, impatient, or rude to you. They may be dealing with losing a loved one or their job, or they might be stressed out to the max at work. Or just having a really bad day.

This has happened to me and taught me such a big lesson regarding how I react in annoying situations with people I encounter whom I don't know at all.

A few years ago, I went to Kohl's department store to look for a new shower curtain liner, as ours was just gross. I couldn't take a shower and look at the yucky curtain any longer.

If you've never been to a Kohl's, let me tell you a little about it. In each department the aisles are very narrow between rows and stacks of stuff. Even their shopping carts are very narrow and tiny (makes sense, I guess). I went early on a Sunday morning, and the store wasn't busy at all. I was in the bathroom accessories section, staring at the shower curtain liners selection, with my back up against the stacked towels behind me. I was looking and looking, taking my time to select the right liner. Did I want the clear or frosted kind?

Then a woman came up near me pushing a cart and asked me to move out of the way so she could pass through. This is how the conversation went.

WOMAN: Can you please move so I can pass through?

I looked around and saw literally no one else in our vicinity, with many alternate routes for this woman to pass by.

ME: Why can't you just go around me that other way?
WOMAN: Because I'm asking you to move so I can
pass this way.
ME: Really, lady? Fine. I'll move.

I started to back up to get out of the way, but then I looked
at the woman's face one more time and saw that she looked
very upset. Why was I such a putz? Yeah, she was annoying,
but now I felt bad.

ME: Ummm. Are you OK? I'm really sorry that I was
so rude to you.
WOMAN: I'm sorry too. My mom just passed away
last night and I had to get a few things this morning to wear to the funeral. I'm in such a daze. I'm
just walking all around through this store.

Holy sh*t. I couldn't believe I upset this woman, who was
clearly having the worst bad day that I could imagine. And all
because I didn't feel like moving out of the way? What was
wrong with me?

We talked for a few minutes. I asked about her mom. She
told me how the last few days had been so stressful, draining,
and sad as her mom was dying.

At the end we hugged each other and I wished her well. She
was so nice to me too.

Now *that* was a lesson that has stuck with me for years.
Don't judge people. Or try not to judge people. You really never
know. It's definitely not "right" that they are being rude, but if
you fight back, push back, you will only escalate their stress
and the situation. But if you take a moment to calm yourself
and have empathy and show kindness, I guarantee the situation will be diffused and you may even be surprised at the
outcome. You have the power to turn their really bad day into

something a bit better and leave that person with a good feeling in their heart.

Try to err on the side of empathy, kindness, and compassion.

MAKE EYE CONTACT AND SMILE—IT WON'T KILL YOU

When you walk down the street and pass someone, do you typically look straight ahead or look sideways to avoid looking that person in the eye? Or do you look at them and smile?

I tend to smile at people most of the time. But I definitely have days when I just look ahead.

When someone smiles at you, it is very hard not to smile back. It's even harder to turn away or frown. There is actual science behind it. Neuroscientist Marco Iacoboni explains that when you smile at someone, you activate their mirror neurons, an automatic response in the brain linked to a mirrored action. The other person often starts to smile without having to think about their response. They feel your smile as if they are smiling themselves, which they often then do.

We don't need to know another person to brighten their day. And it can feel pretty good.

How about when we pass someone who is homeless or begging for money? We sometimes try to ignore the situation, like they aren't really there. I used to do this myself. Why? For fear that they would ask me for money. And what if I didn't have any small bills or loose change on me? Or I didn't feel like giving it to them at that moment? Or I was in a pissy mood?

We often deal with unpleasant situations by resisting them. *If I just ignore it, it's not really happening or there.* Right? We want to escape rather than confront, or God forbid, engage.

One particular situation made me realize that I didn't need to block myself off when passing someone homeless. Because, quite frankly, I always felt like a total schmuck after I walked by and ignored the person, regardless if they asked me for money or not. I have even doubled back occasionally, changing my mind that, yes, I had a dollar I could give them.

One thing I realized was that I didn't need to shut myself off completely and pretend this person didn't exist. I could literally just smile.

Here's my story.

My kids and husband decided to get a dog after we left Singapore. Actually, the kids decided it would be their "gift" from me for making them move back to New Jersey. Not that I thought they warranted a gift after I had given them two years of amazing experiences living and traveling in Asia. But that's another story.

I was vehemently opposed to getting a dog, as I didn't grow up with one and wasn't comfortable around them. I wouldn't let a dog lick me (or at least I tried to avoid it!), and never ever could I imagine picking up poo. Yuck. Gross. Never.

As I dug in my heels and said there was no way we were getting a dog, the kids became more creative in their arguments. They were pretty smart and leveraged what they knew of me. Yes, my children may have picked up some marketing skills from their mom—specifically, understanding the consumer.

One of their arguments was "Mom, think of all the new people you will meet when you walk the dog." To which I told them, I didn't want to meet any new people. I had enough friends. But thank you very much.

I'm still not sure if I ever really said yes to getting a dog. But over time, they wore me down and I stopped saying no so vehemently.

One day we picked up Thomas, a fifteen-pound Newfie (Newfoundland) puppy, and welcomed him into our home. I slowly learned not to be afraid of dogs, and as Thomas grew, so did my love for him. (FYI, he is now 155 pounds of pure love, drool, and joy.)

And the kids were totally right about their consumer insight. One of the key benefits for me of having a dog was talking to new people, strangers, on the street. They were bang on. Smart kids.

I would take Thomas into town for a walk and, because he's so darn cute and there aren't many Newfies around, inevitably I couldn't walk a couple feet (or even steps) without people stopping me to ask the same questions over and over.

"What kind of dog is that?"

"How much does he weigh?"

"What's his name?"

I loved interacting with people. Often they offered up stories of their own dog, or shared memories of a dog they used to have. I looked forward to these walks and meeting new people. The best part was seeing smiles on people's faces. We even had cars slow down, or those stopped at traffic lights roll down their windows to say hi and smile. Once a young man on a scooter backtracked to say hi and get a sloppy, wet kiss from Thomas.

Then I started to notice a pattern. As we walked along, about 90 percent of people would smile, and these people would want to stop and ask to pet Thomas, or just ask me questions. Then there were the 10 percent who, as we approached one another, would tense up and look scared sh*tless upon seeing my enormous dog, who really does look like a bear. And I would try to hold Thomas back, as he loves people and kissing everyone, so they wouldn't be afraid.

As the months went by, I started to notice something else on our walks in town. We have quite a few churches in our small town that serve meals to the homeless. We also have the Market Street Mission, which is located right next to our one and only Starbucks. Many people who rely on the churches and mission for their daily meals and shelter can be seen walking through town or waiting outside of the churches or Starbucks between getting their meals.

I noticed as I walked Thomas through town that they would smile at us but then look away and rarely, if ever, strike up a conversation or ask me those favorite questions that most people ask. And none of them would ask if they could pet him.

I thought this was odd, so I started to do something different than just smile and walk by. I would stop and ask them if they would like to pet Thomas. Bright smiles and resounding yeses. Then the same inevitable questions would flow.

"What kind of dog is that?"

"How much does he weigh?"

"What's his name?"

And then they would often share stories of their own dogs they grew up with.

By simply smiling at someone homeless you can make a small yet meaningful connection. It's recognition that they haven't been forgotten.

I shared my observations with my family. I asked (really told) my kids and husband that when they were walking Thomas in town I wanted them to walk slower in front of the churches and Market Street Mission, and ask the people standing out front if they would like to say hi to Thomas. We have the opportunity to share and bring so much joy to people.

Being friendly and kind to people I encounter daily, smiling more, making eye contact, and, yes, even talking to strangers makes me happy. I know I always feel good when I interact with others in a positive way.

> Kindness reminds others of their value,
>   their importance to this world.
> Kindness has the power to uplift, refill,
>   encourage and renew.

> —Tamara Letter, *A Passion for Kindness*

YOU DON'T HAVE TO BE A BYSTANDER

I can't remember the first time I heard of the "bystander effect," but I've definitely seen it in action. The bystander effect is essentially the phenomenon that occurs when there is an emergency situation and people don't intervene because others are present. The individual doesn't take action because either they think that someone else will and they don't feel as much pressure to do something themselves, or they feel that maybe it's not appropriate for them to do something, as others are probably more qualified to help. During a crisis, things are often chaotic and the situation is not always crystal clear. Onlookers might wonder exactly what is happening. During such chaotic moments, people often look to others in the group to determine what is appropriate. When people look at the crowd and see that no one else is reacting, it sends a signal that perhaps no action is needed.

As I have mentioned earlier, we are so acclimatized to not picking up strangers in our cars. I think that we are so paranoid and overly cautious that we have lost some of our will to interact and help out people who are strangers.

For example, imagine you see an accident on the road. Or you notice a car is on the side of the highway with the driver standing outside. Perhaps a flat tire? Or they spun out? Do you stop and help? Is it safe to do so? We've all watched horror movies and know how that could end!

But what if you simply pulled over to the side of the road and backed up safely? Don't get out of your car, but roll down your window and ask the person if you can call for roadside assistance for them. Do they need water?

You have to be safe and protect yourself, but what if it was *you* or someone in your family who was in this situation? Wouldn't you want some good Samaritan to stop and ask if you needed help?

Quite a few years ago, my parents came to visit us in New Jersey. We went to the Willowbrook Mall together, the kids running up and down the corridors as we ducked in and out of stores. As per usual, my dad had "had enough." He's always been terrific with my kids, but after playing with them for some time, he needs a break.

> DAD: Guys, I've had enough.
> MOM: Stanley, come on, keep walking with us.
> DAD: No, I've had enough. I'm going to go buy a coffee and then sit and read my paper over there by that fountain.

He pointed to the large fountain like those that you typically see in a shopping mall, with the shallow water that people throw loose change into. I'm not sure if these still exist today, but back in the day they provided countless minutes of enjoyment for kids, who threw pennies in while their parents took a breather from running around the mall with them.

> MOM: OK, suit yourself.

This is one of my mother's favorite refrains. What does one do with "suit yourself"? Is it permission to really do what you want? Or is it said with such a tone that if you do have the courage to "suit yourself," you feel guilty as you are doing it?

And off we went in our different directions. After about forty-five minutes, we returned to the meeting spot at the fountain.

> MOM: Stanley, why are you all wet? What's wrong with you?
> DAD: I was reading my paper and looked up to take a sip of my coffee and saw that this little boy was

facedown in the water in the fountain. I looked up and around and no one else seemed to notice him. So I walked into the fountain and lifted the little boy out.

What a mensch! We were all so proud of him. My mom quickly forgot that he had abandoned us and gave him a point or two.

Another time, while living in Singapore, I decided to refresh my CPR skills, as I hadn't done a course since my daughter was born fourteen years before. I signed up to do a First Aid/CPR course with the Singapore Red Cross that took place over two weekends.

At home I would practice my new "skills" on my kids, bandaging them for hypothetical burns and cuts, doing the moves for Heimlich and CPR. The drill always started the way they told you to do it. You approached the victim and said, "Hi, my name is Elisa and I'm a first responder." Then you did your thing, according to the steps. Two weeks later, I got certified and proudly carried my Singapore Red Cross card in my wallet.

Not too long after I finished the course, we went on a family vacation to India. We had just arrived at the grand Taj Mahal, walking through the entrance and pausing for a few minutes to look in awe at it from a distance. Then right in front of us, a young woman fell to the ground and let out a scream. She had been taking photos on the grass beside the paved path and didn't notice there was barbed wire between the grass and the path and thus tripped and landed on the barbed wire.

I immediately ran over to her and saw blood streaming from her chin. I yelled for Kobi and Adam to come help me get her up, and we moved her to a bench. She had cuts on her legs as well, but was bleeding a lot from her chin. I removed the shirt I had tied around my waist and used it to apply pressure to her chin. A couple of people started to gather and watch. They literally formed a small semicircle around us. Most others looked at us and then kept walking toward the Taj Mahal. Could any of these people who walked by have been more trained or adept at helping this woman? Most likely, yes. But I'll never know.

I started to shout out to anyone who could hear me for water and tissues or any other cloth to help control the bleeding. I distinctly remember one person gave us a bottle of water and that was it. Even our own tour guide stood back and watched.

After the injured woman settled a bit and I was applying pressure to her chin, putting water on the cuts on her arms and legs, I asked her if she was with someone. She said that she was by herself and had a driver waiting outside the entrance. She described the driver and we had our guide go out and find him. Adam and Kobi helped her walk to the waiting car, and the injured woman and her driver went off to get her medical attention.

After she left, my kids turned to me and said, "Mom, you did something very wrong. You didn't start with 'My name is Elisa and I'm a first responder.'"

What a couple of smart-asses.

I learned a couple of things from this experience. Number one is that in an actual situation versus a practice demonstration in class, we aren't always going to get everything right. And number two is that, in retrospect, I should have been more careful protecting myself when touching her because of all the blood. I reacted quickly, but I could have taken other shirts from people to cover my hands as I applied the pressure to her deep gash.

A couple of years later, another situation presented itself to me.

My friends Lynn and Erik were visiting from Quebec and I took them to our nearby park, Jockey Hollow, to go for a walk with Thomas. As we were driving back home, the traffic slowed completely in front of us. We saw a motorcycle on its side in the middle of the road, and off the side of the road just ahead it looked like someone was on the ground with a couple of people standing around.

I pulled the car over and said to my friends that I was just going to see if they needed any help. As I approached the scene, I saw maybe five people standing in a semicircle around the fallen motorcycle driver. I asked if anyone had called 911. They had.

But they were all just standing there. No one was talking to the young injured motorcyclist. So I knelt down beside him and asked him his name. He was in pain and trying to move. I knew that I was supposed to keep him from moving and getting up until the emergency people arrived. So I sat and talked to him. I asked him if he lived with anyone. He said he lived with his dad. I called up to the people standing around us and asked someone to get their phone out. The motorcyclist gave us his dad's number and the bystander called his dad for him. As he was still trying to move, I tried to keep him talking, asking if he had any pets (he had a dog). Then the paramedics arrived and took over. It was only maybe five minutes from when I got there.

The bystanders did the right thing. They called 911 for help and then stayed at the scene until help arrived. But why didn't any of them bend down to talk to the injured motorcyclist?

Don't worry, my friends, I'm not suggesting you run to catch a baby out of a fiery apartment window. Not being a bystander need not be as heroic as this example. It's as simple as when you notice someone needs assistance, you step in rather than just walk past them. That's being a true mensch.

I'm not sure about doing "big gestures" but I always seek to be kind to those around me. This could mean offering to help someone with a pram on the underground, or helping an old person carry a suitcase upstairs. I recently helped a lady who was in tears of pain as she had sprained her ankle and could barely walk. My dad and I helped her off the train and through the station. (George K.)

I picked up a mother and child who were walking home on a bitterly cold, windy day and drove them home. The mom was so grateful. (Elayne I.)

If I ever see anyone who is experiencing difficulty of some sort, in a store, at the bank, or on the street, I will usually offer up assistance if I am able. It takes very little effort to be nice. (Teri R.)

WHEN TRAGEDY STRIKES ON A BIG LEVEL

Disasters, earthquakes, tsunamis, school shootings, COVID-19—when these things hit, we are bombarded with images, news, and stories. But it is happening to *them*, not *us*, right? We can sit on our sofa watching the TV or read the news on our phones. It's tragic and sad. We watch stories of how individuals are impacted and we may feel a connection to them. There's empathy. But really, is it our place to help? Don't they have their own local governments, communities, and organizations already helping? And even if we wanted to, what could we really do? If we donated money, would it really be used in an impactful way?

But what if it happened to us? In our community? Wouldn't we want as many people as possible around the world to help us? We can, each of us, do our part to help others whom we do not know, but who we know are suffering. We can do our little part to help ease their suffering and simultaneously feel good about doing something versus nothing.

Ask yourself, *What can I do to help?* When a disaster hits, we see fundraising campaigns rise up from the Red Cross and other relief organizations. We don't have to give at the same levels as Warren Buffett or Bill and Melinda Gates. Donating even twenty-five dollars to a cause will help, and it will give us that helper's high too. We've done something, not nothing.

I wrote much of this book as the COVID-19 crisis hit us, while we were on stay-at-home orders in New Jersey. I witnessed so many grassroots initiatives sprouting right here in little Morristown, New Jersey. Regular, ordinary people taking the initiative to rally others in our community to join in.

In the beginning, I felt so hopeless. While I was safe in my own home, people were getting sick and dying in my community, across the country, around the world. And what could I do? I wasn't a doctor or a nurse. What could *I* really do?

Then I started to see new Facebook groups show up on my feed. People in my community were organizing to help. The Morristown Order Out Twice a Week Stimulus Plan to support our local restaurants, Morristown Helps to support our hospital workers. I now had a focal point of places that I could visit online and help make a small difference.

All I can say is: do the best you can with what you have. And we all have something to give.

RANDOM ACTS OF KINDNESS

What would a book about helping others, being a mensch, be without a chapter on random acts of kindness?

A random act of kindness is an unexpected act of helping someone or simply doing a kind deed. GoodTherapy.org explains, "The term random act of kindness is generally attributed to Anne Herbert, who wrote, 'Practice random kindness and senseless acts of beauty' on a restaurant place mat. The term refers to selfless acts, both large and small, that are committed unexpectedly, without prompting and with no apparent ulterior motive."[7]

It feels so good when someone does something nice for us that totally comes out of the blue. And it also feels so good when we do something nice for others that is spontaneous, unexpected. The helper's high is very powerful. You may get an immediate reaction from the person, or if you do something for someone and they don't see you, you walk or drive away with a huge smile on your face. It's so cool either way.

MENSCH THINGS YOU CAN DO

- Pay for the coffee of the person behind you in line.
- Hold the door open for someone.
- Give another person a store coupon you aren't using.
- Give a paid parking ticket to the next person parking in your spot if you haven't used up all the time.
- Send flowers to a friend just because.

---

7. https://www.goodtherapy.org/blog/psychpedia/random-act-of-kindness, accessed April 15, 2020.

- Tip BIG!
- Offer to hold the bags of an elderly person or someone with a baby while they cross the street, or load their groceries into their car for them.
- Shovel your neighbor's driveway the morning after a snowstorm.

I held a lady's baby while she was boarding a plane since she was having a hard time with the stroller and carrying the baby, so I just took over and helped her while I saw many before me just pass her by. (Natalia Y.)

I just bought a service member's lunch. With two active-duty family members, it was my way of doing something for them by proxy. (Tara T.)

I was in a parking garage last week and a man walked over to my car and gave me his parking ticket because he paid for two hours but only used fifteen minutes of it! It was a small gesture but made me very happy. (Sherry D.)

You CAN help people you don't know and show your awesome kindness. Use your sekhel and assess the situation to decide what you can do. There is always something and it doesn't need to be heroic. The smallest act of kindness can have a great impact on the person who is receiving it.

CHAPTER FIVE

The *Kinde*, They Can Make Us So Proud

When I was growing up, every Friday night my family would have Shabbat dinner together. My bubbie, mom, dad, Auntie Nina, Uncle Jack, and all the kinde. My mom and aunt were pretty smart about how they got us to show up for Shabbat dinner every week as we got older and wanted to go out with friends instead of having a family meal on the *weekend*. We needed to be at dinner, but could go out with our friends afterward. And with this agreement in place, almost every Shabbat dinner my brothers and cousins and I would be there together.

It was always someone's job to pick up Bubbie Regina with the huge pot of chicken soup she made for dinner. We all knew that we couldn't arrive before 5:25 p.m. because she needed to finish watching *The Young and the Restless*. When we got up to her apartment and she opened the door, she was always ready to go. Lipstick on, nails impeccable, and the huge pot of soup resting on the stovetop.

When it was my turn to pick up Bubbie Regina, she would recap the latest episode of *The Young and the Restless* with me on the seven-minute drive to my parents' or aunt and uncle's house, whoever's house we were gathering at that night. I'm not sure if my brothers and cousins had similar conversations, but I always looked forward to the recap, as I had often missed the episode due to being at work.

Holidays like Rosh Hashanah (Jewish New Year) and Passover involved Bubbie making more of her traditional foods. As she got older and her arthritis got worse, we were summoned (really, instructed) to go help Bubbie, especially with the gefilte fish. Our job was to help her stir the raw fish mixture, as it was too heavy and difficult for her to do herself.

This is how the decision was made on which of us was to have the job of helping Bubbie at any given holiday. I always had this picture in my head of my mom and aunt with two cardboard tubes from toilet paper rolls connected by a piece of string running from one house to the other, so they could communicate twenty times a day. A direct line. They lived less than a ten-minute drive apart but were always on the phone with each other throughout the day.

MOM: Nacha, who is going to help Mama make the
    fish this week?
AUNTIE NINA: Send one of the boys. Elisa has the
    little kids and she's going to come early to help us
    before dinner too.
MOM: Good idea. Which one?
AUNTIE NINA: Well, Benji has exams this week,
    David and Yosi helped me bring up the Passover
    dishes, and Avrum helped Mama just last week.
MOM: That leaves Jamie. Yes, I think it's his turn
    this week.
AUNTIE NINA: OK, let's send Jamie over.

You see, my brothers, cousins, and I grew up with expectations from our moms. Expectations to help our bubbie, help around the house and do chores, and help others. It was ingrained in us—not a choice but a "this is what you are going to do." Most of the time we pushed back at first when they would ask us. Don't all kids do that? And we felt that our moms' expectations were particularly high, sometimes unreasonable even. Usually though, we succumbed and did what they asked us to do.

I don't remember exactly when they started to show us the way to being kind to others, or told us explicitly, but it was always there.

WHEN I BECAME A PARENT MYSELF

When I wrote down my goals with my life coach a few years ago, one of them was "to raise my kids to be good contributors to society." In other words, to raise my kids to be mensches. This was really important to me. I acknowledged that my kids were being raised with so many privileges, more than most kids. After all, how many American or Canadian kids lived in Singapore and traveled all throughout Asia?

The first time I went on a plane with my own parents was when I was eighteen years old and we went on a family trip to Disney World in Orlando, Florida. Before then, the few trips we took were road trips. My parents sent us to overnight summer camp, which we loved and was really expensive, so trips throughout the year were very seldom.

Yet here I was, flying around the world with my own kids. I wanted to make sure that they knew this was special, and that they appreciated all that they had. But how to do this? To ensure it really happened? I wanted them to always keep in mind that they had an obligation to be kind and help others less fortunate.

I'm no parenting expert. Far from it. But I read a lot, talk to my friends, and of course seek guidance from my mom and aunt. This is what I've learned along my journey as I'm doing my best to navigate parenthood.

The research I've found talks about how children who are kind are happier and more connected and compassionate. They will have what they need to become change makers in the world. Make the world a better place.

As Tamara Letter states in her book *A Passion for Kindness: Making the World a Better Place to Lead, Love, and Learn*, "Children who are raised in a culture where giving and compassion are valued become happier and more positively engaged with those around them. They are less likely to treat others disrespectfully. Research shows that when you talk to your kids about giving to others, and provide them with opportunities to do so, they are more likely to be happy and have a positive influence on the world. Even the smallest gesture of kindness communicates to someone that we respect and value them. As we model kindness for our children, and offer them their own opportunities to practice it, they will become more open to and understanding of others."[8]

Now, telling your kids that if they are kind and compassionate they will be happier probably won't do the trick. You have to be more creative in ways that you demonstrate and talk to your kids so that the outcome is what you strive for.

There are countless opportunities to discuss and demonstrate kindness to your kids. It's not a "one and done" type of thing. What I've found is that it's more about nurturing a spirit of kindness in the daily life of your kids. And you'll see

---

8. *A Passion for Kindness: Making the World a Better Place to Lead, Love, and Learn* by Tamara Letter.

moments when your kids are doing real mensch-like things. But they will also do things that you're not happy with. That's just life. That's just kids.

KIDS CAN BE A PAIN IN THE TUCHES, BUT THEY DO HAVE THEIR SHINING MOMENTS

Kids can be a royal pain in the butt. Tantrums as toddlers, constantly asking us to buy things for them, do things for them. And yet when we ask them to do something, they don't always do it immediately, or ever. They get all *ongeblozen*. Sound familiar?

> **ongeblozen**
> /un-geh-BLUH-zin/
> *adj.* sulky, pouty

But sometimes there are moments that we see them do something remarkably kind. Nothing warms a parent's heart more than observing their kid doing something nice for someone else. In Yiddish, we call this *shepping naches*.

> **shep naches**
> /shep NA-ches/
> *v.* to derive pleasure

Here is a story of when not only I but my mom and aunt *shepped naches* from my daughter.

My parents never had a nanny for us growing up—neither live-in nor live-out. We did have a cleaning lady who came for a few hours every two weeks, but that was it. My mom was a big believer in us doing chores, so my brothers and I all knew how to vacuum and dust, and we had mastered the critical life skill of ironing sheets, pillowcases, and underwear.

The first and only time my parents hired a live-in nanny was when my bubbie was no longer able to live independently and moved in with them. They hired a wonderful caregiver, Orly, to help take care of my bubbie as she was ailing in her final year of life. Bubbie got my former bedroom upstairs. The furniture from her apartment was moved in to make her more comfortable.

We continued to have Shabbat dinners every Friday night with our family: my brothers, their wives, my aunt and uncle, and my cousins and their partners, who would eventually all become their wives. When we sat down to eat, one of us was always upstairs keeping my bubbie company as she was too frail to join us downstairs. I don't remember this being something explicit that my mom or aunt asked us to do—we just did it. On Friday night one of us would say, "I'll stay with Bubbie upstairs during dinner and then eat afterward."

After a few of these Friday nights, my daughter Sydnee, who was three-and-a-half years old at the time, told us that she was going to sit with Bubbie that night during dinner. She started to lug in a little table and chair that my parents had for the little kids in a different bedroom and set up her area right beside Bubbie's bed. We all told her that she should come downstairs to eat with us and *then* she could visit with Bubbie afterward. But we were to find out that Sydnee could be as determined and stubborn as her mom, my mom, and my aunt. So we relented. And from then on, Sydnee took it upon herself that it was her turn to sit with Bubbie every Shabbat dinner.

NU, TELL ME, HOW DO WE RAISE OUR KIDS TO BE MENSCHES?

I really do not believe there is a magic answer to this question. It is a lot of trial and error. What I can offer you are some suggestions of things you can do with your kids that I have experienced myself with great results (and a lot of patience, deep breaths, and perhaps a glass or two of wine).

Try to Behave Like Mensches Ourselves

Kids are sponges. They watch what we do and imitate it. Remember when your kids played dress-up and got into your makeup drawer, trying to be like you? Or when they were toddlers learning to speak, you'd hear YOUR words coming out of their mouths? You would hear them say to a younger sibling, "I'm going to count to three if you don't give me that toy."

The most horrifying is the first time they swear as a two-year-old when you're out in public with them. You are aghast. Where did my kid learn to speak that way? Hmmm . . . You probably know. You are terribly embarrassed, but also kind of secretly proud that they used that swear word in the proper context. (I know I was.)

As they get older, it may not be as obvious that your kids are paying any attention to you at all. They are so absorbed in their devices, iPads, video games, and phones as they get old enough to have their own. But believe me, they do continue to watch you closely. They keep tabs on what you say and your behavior. And yes, they do eventually act in ways that are similar to how *you* act, mimicking your quirks and behaviors just like they did when they were little kids.

Our kids also watch how we treat others, whether they comment on it or not. Typically they will comment when it is something embarrassing you do, such as if you approach a couple on the street who look lost—and maybe are arguing a bit—and offer directions. "Mom, don't go over there. It's not your business. You are sooooo embarrassing!"

They see you help an elderly person load their groceries into their car or see you leaving the house to go volunteer. They may not say anything, but believe me, they are watching, observing. And it does sink in. (We hope.) Your kids will watch how you interact with others. How you treat servers at a restaurant if you are waiting an extra-long time for your food to arrive. Do you get really short with the server and say in a stern tone, "We've been waiting *thirty* minutes for our meals. Our kids are hungry"? Or do you call over the server and say in a normal voice, "Excuse me, when do you think our meals will be ready? Can you please check with the kitchen?"

Or you are leaving the grocery store in a hurry with the kids in tow, already running late to their practice. You spy an elderly man struggling to put his groceries in his car. Do you glance at him, then keep walking to your car? Or, do you approach the man and tell him you are just going to put your kids in the car then will be back in a second to help him?

This may be a simple thing, but I remember the first time I saw one of my kids offering up their seat on the subway to an elderly person. I was about to do it myself, but then my daughter beat me to it. She just stood up and quietly asked the person if they would like her seat.

Wow.

Talk with Our Kids

Most of the time I feel like I'm talking *to* my kids instead of talking *with* them. Here's a likely familiar conversation at the dinner table.

ME: How was school today?
KOBI: Good.

ME: What did you do?

KOBI: Stuff.

ME: Who did you sit with at lunch?

KOBI: Mom, I'm eating. Can you just leave me alone?

It's typically at the dinner table when I have an opportunity to have their attention. It's a short window, that's for sure. If I see that they may be in a more open mood to talk, then I take that opportunity and go for it.

I try to share with my kids when I do something kind or I hear of people doing something nice for others. I don't do it to boast to them, but rather to give them ideas, so that when a situation arises they have these ideas and thoughts in their minds already to tap into and act upon. I'll talk about something that has recently occurred, either an incident in our community or a big news event, and ask them their thoughts. Sometimes I think that what I say falls onto deaf ears, but other times we actually have a discussion.

They may engage in the discussion, even ask questions. Or they may be silent and you think nothing got through to them. Then you observe or hear from someone else about your kid doing a wonderful, kind act, and voilà! It's like osmosis. It *did* get through to them!

What's most amazing is when you do get those glorious moments when your kids are actually engaging with you, and you hear their opinions on things and how their voices are emerging.

Make Kids Do Things They Don't Want to Do

You heard me right. Make your kids do things they don't want to do. But not for nothing. Not for the sport of it. When it's something that you think will be good for them, be strong and push forward. It's hard when your kids don't listen to you—and I personally give up much of the time. It takes way too much energy to keep on nagging them. And I hate hearing my own voice nagging too. The kids probably think I get enjoyment out of nagging them. They don't realize that I hate this activity as much as they do.

And then explain why you are making them do it. They will push back, maybe even throw a tantrum. Why? Because they are bad kids who are self-centered? Maybe a bit of that is true. But the underlying reason sometimes is that they are uncomfortable with what is being asked of them.

It's our job to try as much as we can to keep calm in these situations and try to unearth what is behind the reason that they don't want to do something. It could be that they just don't feel like it, they don't see the benefit for themselves, or they are scared and uncomfortable. Every situation has a different reason and it's impossible to figure it all out. But we can try our best.

Be Creative in How We Get Our Kids to Do Things

I learned from the masters on this one. My mom and aunt had really creative ways to get us to do things.

As kids get older, they are constantly growing out of their clothes and no longer playing with all the toys they played with when they were younger. And the mess piles up everywhere. As much as you try, you can't keep up with tidying or getting them to help you clean up. You finally have had it and decide you are going to get them to help you sort through everything and then donate.

My kids are not big fans when I ask them to do this. So what I do is, rather than nag continuously about the mess, I focus more on that I'm asking them to clean up, to sort through their things so we can donate what they don't want to kids who are less fortunate. By giving them another reason, it helps. But don't think this is an immediate solution. No way. It still takes some nagging, until I'm actually in their room with the bags, ready to sort with them.

My son Kobi grew something like seven inches the year right after his Bar Mitzvah, when he was thirteen. I had bought him a very nice suit for his own Bar Mitzvah and then multiple pairs of nice pants, button-down shirts, and ties that he could wear to his friends' Bar Mitzvahs and Bat Mitzvahs. As you can imagine, he grew out of all these clothes pretty quickly.

I didn't want to pack them up in a bag and drop it into a Goodwill bin or another bin that accepted used clothing. For me, I felt these clothes required extra-special care, and I wanted to make sure that the kids who received them got them in good condition, so they would feel good about wearing them versus wearing someone else's discards.

I called Kobi's middle school, and after discussing with the person who organized all the clothing donations, we realized that Kobi's clothes that he had outgrown were going to be too big for the average middle schooler. We've got tall genes in the family. As I mentioned earlier, my husband is six feet five, his dad was six feet seven at his tallest, and my side of the family isn't short either. My dad is six feet three, my brother Jamie is six feet two, and my "short" brother Avrum is almost six feet.

I didn't give up there. I called the high school, where they had a program I'd heard about called Colonial Closet. (The Morristown Colonials are our high school mascots.) The woman I spoke with at the high school told me that they were no longer running the program. I was disappointed and told her about the "fancy" clothes I had to donate. She then had the idea that for high school graduation photos many of the students didn't have their own shirt, tie, and nice pants. The school had a couple of nice shirts that they would lend the boys for the graduation photos. Kobi's clothes would be a perfect addition, and I was welcome to drop those off to her directly at the school. She would make sure they were given to boys around graduation photo time.

It was a beautiful idea that I could totally get behind. I then told Kobi that's what we were going to do and he got behind it as well. Much to his chagrin, he tried on all his clothes for me to inspect that they were too small for him. Yes, I made him try everything on.

I then explained to Kobi that we were going to wash everything, iron the clothes, and then put them on hangers. We weren't going to throw everything into bags. When he went to get dressed for a Bar Mitzvah he wouldn't want to have to put on crumpled, dirty clothes out of a bag, would he? We were going to make sure his clothes looked really nice, like they came from a store, for these kids at the high school whose parents couldn't afford to buy them new clothes like I did for him.

Over the years, I've done the same thing with both my kids, making them sort through their toys and books and then taking them with me to the library or day care center to donate so they could see the new home for all their stuff.

Nice Things for Them, Nice Things for Others Too

Another way to foster kindness in your kids is when you do nice things for your kids, incorporate how they can do nice things for other people at the same time. Show them the win-win. Making your kids a part of the experience in helping others gives them a feeling of connection and purpose that they can't learn any other way.

HERE ARE A FEW IDEAS ON WHAT WE CAN DO WITH OUR KIDS

- When kids are younger, a cool thing to do for part of their Hanukkah or Christmas gift is to help them sponsor a child in need. There are many organizations, such as Brillo de Sol (a school for developmentally and physically challenged kids in Guatemala), World Vision, and Save the Children, where your child can be partnered with a child in need. Your sponsorship can be paying for the other child's education, food, and other basic necessities. Part of these programs often includes your child and the recipient becoming pen pals, exchanging drawings and letters.

- Have your kids donate from their birthday celebrations. There are cool websites like ECHOage that you can use when you are sending out the birthday invitations to their friends. Instead of giving your kid a birthday gift, you can ask people to donate to ECHOage. Half the money raised is for the birthday kid to buy a gift—whatever they would like. Then the birthday kid chooses a charity or other organization they are interested in, such as helping animals, the environment, or other kids, and the other half of the money raised is donated to that organization.

- For teens celebrating a communion, quinceañera, Sweet 16, Bar Mitzvah, or Bat Mitzvah who receive monetary gifts, consider having your child donate a percentage of the money they receive to a charitable organization of their choice.

- If trays of food are left over after their party, engage your kids to help you pack it up and drop it off at a food-rescue organization or homeless shelter in your community.

Incorporate Service into Travel

When we started to travel more with our kids when we lived in Singapore, they were the perfect age, I thought, at ten and twelve years old, to start involving them in giving back while we traveled. I wanted to give them the opportunity to see how people lived in other places around the world, and travel was a really good way to do this.

Let me tell you a story of one of the times that I put thought and effort into building this into our vacation and what happened.

My husband and I had already visited India separately for business trips, but we hadn't been on a vacation there as a family. From a young age, our kids loved Indian food and so we knew that would be a bonus for them going there and we wouldn't have issues like many other people whose kids were picky eaters.

I planned our trip with the help of a recommended travel agent who offered bespoke itineraries. "Bespoke" was the new fancy word I learned in Singapore that basically means customized. I love that word. The travel agent offered suggestions for the main tourist sites in the Golden Triangle of Delhi, Agra, and Jaipur. I then asked that she help me incorporate visiting a place where we could volunteer as a family and/or donate to.

Our itinerary finalized, we had an amazing array of iconic sites such as the Red Fort, Taj Mahal, Agra Fort, palaces, and bazaars. Built into our itinerary were visits to Mother Teresa's Missionaries of Charity home in Agra and the Ladli Vocational Training Center for Women in Jaipur.

With our itinerary set, I got busy buying school supplies and little toys to give to these organizations when we visited: coloring books, coloring markers and pencils, and everything under the sun that I thought the kids would like. I packed it all up into its own suitcase to bring with us.

The beginning of our trip was wonderful and everything I could have hoped for. We spent the first couple of days in Delhi and then made our way to Agra, where we saw the majestic Taj Mahal. The kids were amazing. As I expected, they loved the food and were great travelers.

Then the day came for our visit to the first organization, the Mother Teresa orphanage. I separated the things we brought to donate into two large bags and off we went with our local guide in his van.

Our guide had the address, and when we got there, he looked quizzically at me in the back seat. The building was nondescript and there were not very many cars parked out front, and literally not a soul to be seen outside the building. He asked me if this was the right place. I told him I had no idea; I wasn't from Agra, let alone India!

The thing is that we hadn't booked a specific tour of Mother Teresa's Missionaries of Charity homes. I had thought (mistakenly) that our tour operator who had added it to our tour had actually contacted them and/or knew we could visit. All we had was the name and address on our itinerary and off we went. To be honest, I think on our itinerary it may have just been written "Mother Teresa Orphanage." Maybe it was a local home instead of the main place? I didn't do my research, so I really didn't know.

I told our guide to just park and I would go up to the door. So with the bag of donations in hand, I approached the door and knocked. Then knocked again. And again. Finally, the door creaked open a bit, and standing there was a little old nun.

ME: Good afternoon. Is this the Mother Teresa orphanage?

NUN: (Nodding yes.)

ME: Can we please come in to visit you?

NUN: (Gives me a blank look.)

ME: Where are the children?

NUN: They are resting.

ME: We brought some things for the children.

I outstretched my arm with the big bag that I had brought. The nun took the bag, said thank you, and shut the door. *What?*

I walked back to the van, and when I got in, this was the conversation.

SYDNEE: Mom, aren't we going in?

ME: Apparently not. There must have been some mix-up with our travel agent. I think the children are resting now.

KOBI: Wait, no orphans?

ADAM: Where are the orphans, Elisa?

And that became the joke on me for the next couple of days. I felt totally down. I had planned and built up this visit with my family to be a wonderful experience. I did tell them that the important thing was that we gave the donations to children in need. But this wasn't exactly how I had hoped our visit would go. It was not the teaching experience I had anticipated.

Next on our itinerary was Jaipur, also known as the Pink City. We visited the City Palace and Amber Fort and went to a small ceramics factory and workshop to watch how people made the beautiful ceramic bowls we saw in the bazaars.

The day after these sights, the next stop was another organization. This one was called the Ladli Vocational Training

Center in Jaipur. After the little miscommunication about the
Mother Teresa orphanage, I did google this next place, and it
looked like there would be an opportunity to at least see people there. I told Adam and the kids the same, to which they of
course replied, "Sure, Mom, let's go visit more orphans."

We had a different local guide this time around, someone from Jaipur itself. He drove us to the place and as we
approached we saw people and a big sign on the front of the
building reading, THE LADLI VOCATIONAL TRAINING CENTER
FOR ABUSED, ORPHANED AND DESTITUTE GIRLS.

This looked promising.

I told everyone to get out of the van to come in with me.
They wanted to wait in the van and have me go in first to check
it out. But I insisted they join me. I took the second bag of
donations and we walked up.

The door was open and there was a lot of activity inside.
We were in the store/working building, where we saw an array
of handmade crafts displayed and also young women and
teenagers gathered in a circle on the carpet, making crafts.

The people there were so welcoming. They talked to us
about the programs they had for the girls and young women,
showed us the building where the girls lived, and explained
that while the girls went to school their mothers worked making crafts that were sold to companies throughout India and
overseas.

The kids, and even Adam, sat with the women as they
showed them how to weave bracelets. We could have stayed
there for hours. Everyone was enjoying themselves. And I made
sure that while they were having a good time making the
bracelets, they also heard and understood what this wonderful
place was about—giving training to women to earn a living, an
education for the girls, and shelter and food.

Mission accomplished, finally.

Nu, what did I learn from this? It's not going to be perfect. In fact, when *is* travel completely perfect with no mishaps, misadventures? But often what happens is you figure out things along the way and make lemonade out of lemons. From then on, when we incorporated volunteer activities or visiting a local organization, I always did my own research beforehand. I would then show my kids the website, talk to them about where we would be going, and engage them in what they wanted to bring to donate. This way they became active participants instead of just being dragged along by their annoying mom.

And hopefully these experiences and memories would cement in them a passion for giving themselves.

Volunteer When the Kids Are Old Enough

Serving people who are experiencing hard times fosters compassion, empathy, and gratitude in our kids. I have to admit that I rely a lot on my kids' school when it comes to volunteering experiences. And I think the schools do a great job at this— especially in high school, where they are required to complete a certain number of volunteer hours to graduate. The schools provide them with opportunities where they can volunteer if they aren't already doing it on their own.

When my kids were younger, it would be more up to me to find these volunteer opportunities, and I wasn't always so great at being proactive about it. Many organizations required that your kid be at least twelve years old to volunteer with them and interact with recipients of their programs.

We are all busy—especially when raising kids. And we may think we don't have time to volunteer, adding this to school, homework, sports, activities, and our own work and household chores. But volunteering doesn't need to take a lot of time. It doesn't need to be a big, time-consuming effort. Perhaps commit to volunteering as a family once a month, or once every two months. Just think of all that time every day that our kids are on their computers or devices. And let's face it, we are as well.

You could create new traditions in your family. Similar to apple picking every fall, Easter egg hunts, or driving to visit grandparents over Thanksgiving, volunteering together as a family at a specific place will become a family tradition that everyone looks forward to. We can all find a few hours a month away from our devices to commit to a family activity that will bring so many rewards to our children, to our connection as a family, and to others in need.

Teach Kids to Be Kind to (and Maybe Even Help) Strangers

What's the balance between telling your kids not to talk to strangers and also hoping your kids help people in need, who are often strangers?

It can be a gray area and very situation specific. I think the best way to approach this is to always reinforce safety to your kids, but also tell them if they see that someone they don't know needs help, there are always ways to get help. If they aren't with you, but with friends, it could be to notify an adult nearby or use their phone to call for help.

There isn't a blueprint to teach your kids this. Teaching them to tie their shoelaces, or to read, or to clean up their room is much easier. I think that the best way to teach your kids is when the situation arises. They watch how you react and learn from that.

Here is one such example of when the situation presented itself for me and Kobi.

My son had two hockey practices one day with a couple hours between them at the same rink, so I took him to the

McDonald's across the street. When we got there I noticed a middle-aged woman sitting at a table at the front entrance, looking disheveled and a bit "out of it." We walked up to the counter, ordered our food, and ate our dinner at a table closer to the back of the restaurant.

On our way out, I saw that the woman was now lying down on the bench of the table. Kobi and I stopped and I asked her if she was OK. She slurred her words and told us that she was a diabetic and wasn't feeling well. I called over the manager and he called 911.

I had Kobi help me sit her up and we kept her talking so she wouldn't pass out. The ambulance arrived and they took care of her. The manager thanked us for stepping in, as he was more at the "back of the house" and hadn't seen her. He said we could come back anytime and he would treat us to a free dinner.

As we walked out to our car, I talked to Kobi and explained how it's always our job to help people, even if we don't know them and the situation looks a bit "funky." If he was without me and saw something that didn't look right, I told him he should always go seek a manager or another adult to help instead of just walking by.

There are going to be times when you actually teach and guide your kids to help others, and then also times when they do this on their own, and you may not agree completely with what they are doing. This happened in our family on our India trip. We were stuck in traffic in Delhi. And when I say traffic, believe me, you've never seen traffic before like this. We were at a standstill for much of the time. In our van, Adam sat in the front with our local guide, Kobi and I were in the middle, and Sydnee was sitting in the back seat.

Out of the corner of my eye I saw a group of women and girls in the middle of the highway. A young woman motioned to another holding a baby to pass the baby to her. She then walked right over to our van and started to knock on our window, one arm holding the baby, the other with an outstretched hand asking for money. She kept knocking and knocking, propelling the baby forward as she outstretched her hand for money.

Our guide kept calling back to us, "Ignore them. Don't give them money."

Sydnee looked uncomfortable. She said she wanted to give them money. Adam and the guide continued to tell us, "Don't give them money. Look straight ahead. Don't look at them."

I could see that Sydnee was really getting upset. So I reached into my purse and handed her a few rupees. I told her she could do what she wanted.

Sydnee rolled down her window and handed the rupees to the young woman. The woman said thank you, then walked back to her group and passed the baby to another woman.

Now, was that so bad? Many of us judge people who are begging for money, no matter where we live in the world. Some say things like: "By giving them money you are only exacerbating the situation." "They probably have a pimp or someone like that who takes all the money and it's not even going to them." "They will probably buy alcohol with the money, not real food." Haven't we all seen movies like *Slumdog Millionaire*?

My opinion on this subject, which I have voiced to my husband and kids, is that we have never been in a situation ourselves where we have had to ask strangers for money or beg for money on the street. Regardless of how they use it, can you imagine being in that position to have to beg for money? Who knows what their upbringing was like? Did they have all the advantages that we did, the basic stuff like a safe home, a place to sleep, and food to eat every day? Probably not.

When we walk by a homeless person on the street, I talk to my kids about how sad their situation must be, and then I smile at the person, talk for a couple of minutes, and give them a few dollars.

This is just my opinion and how I handle these things. I do what I feel is right in that particular situation and try to be open and not judge.

Teach Our Kids Empathy

One of the things that I worry about is that my kids will be so self-absorbed with all the things they get and do that they won't have empathy for others. I've found that the best way to teach empathy is by practicing it and demonstrating it to my kids in action. Compassionate parents ultimately raise compassionate children.

> *I took my son to visit my father-in-law at the hospital. He was very attentive to his needs. I was so proud to see his empathy and care, especially when my father-in-law was uncomfortable. My son was trying to change his position until he was more comfortable. It was wonderful to see this side of him since most of the time he acts like a typical teenage boy. (Abby B.)*

One of the hardest things for adults to deal with is when someone passes away. Can you imagine how scared and uncomfortable kids must feel?

My mom often took us to condolence visits with her. We never wanted to go. Who would? But by taking us with her, she showed us how to be compassionate and to pay our respects even when it was very scary and uncomfortable.

A shiva or visitation, unlike a funeral, is less formal and is a good opportunity to teach children that death is a reality of life. It is not something to hide from but something that, with time, we must get comfortable with. Simply showing up is often the hardest even for adults. Give kids the practice and get them comfortable with having compassion and not fearing uncomfortable situations.

It is important to stress to kids that going to a shiva or a visitation is not about them. It is not a time to ask for a snack or to let you know that they are tired. It is about the mourners and being there for them. At the same time don't knock them over the head with your well-intended messages. Don't make them do something you see is really hard for them. Simply showing up with you to make a condolence call is a great start. If you see that they are terribly uncomfortable, make it a brief visit and be sure to tell your child/children when you leave the house that you are proud of them for doing a nice thing for someone else.

When my kids were thirteen and fifteen years old, a neighbor of ours died unexpectedly. It was tragic. He left behind his wife and two teenage daughters who went to the same school as my kids. A GoFundMe was organized as an education fund for his kids. My kids completely surprised me by asking if they could donate to the GoFundMe with their own money. And they did.

I asked them to go over to the house with me to pay their respects and they were both very uncomfortable. I told them that we wouldn't stay very long and that I would be with them. I also suggested things they could say. A simple "I'm sorry for your loss." We went over, stayed briefly, and both kids extended their condolences to the mom and her kids.

Now take a deep breath. I know this chapter has not been for the faint of heart. Your blood pressure may have risen as you were reading and thinking about your kids and different situations along the way. It's not easy raising kids. Some may say that parenting is a thankless task. But I beg to differ. It's difficult, but rewarding. And with our best efforts we can and will raise our kids to be mensches when they become adults, leave the proverbial nest, venture out into the world, and, yes, start their first full-time job and bring everything you taught them about values and kindness along with them.

CHAPTER SIX

Be a Mensch at Work

Throughout my career, I've had mostly wonderful managers (and a couple really crappy ones). I've been a good manager (I think), yet definitely had my "moments." For close to twenty years, I worked for a large global organization and lived and worked in Canada, the United States, and Singapore. I had people reporting to me directly and indirectly, both in the same location where I worked and also remotely.

I've seen a lot of good behavior.

And a lot of *putz* behavior too.

I've lost my cool many times and always regretted it afterward. Even though I've apologized when I acted like a putz or a schmuck, it still haunts me. But I've tried to learn from the good and the bad. And move on from there.

Many of us spend most of our waking hours at work. We often see and interact more with people at work than we do with our own families. While I come from a corporate background, what I'm going to talk about equally applies to all types of work environments whether it be an office, a hospital, a restaurant, or a clothing store. Each of us has a "work" persona, separate from the self we show our family and friends. I'm not saying we are completely Jekyll and Hyde—two totally different people—but there are noticeable changes in how we approach and interact with people in different areas of our lives. Why does this happen? Do you even notice this about yourself? I didn't notice or acknowledge it about myself until it was pointed out to me.

I think part of why I had these two separate "Elisas" was what I learned from my dad.

Here's a little background.

While my dad's parents were born in Canada, their parents emigrated from the former Soviet Union and brought their *yiddishkeit* to their new adopted country. My dad grew up in a working class family. His mom, my Bubbie Shirley, was an Avon lady (for fifty years, I might add) and my Zaida Gordon was a bookkeeper. Money was always scarce, but what they lacked in money, they made up for with love. As a young child, my dad was surrounded by love. Based on the stories he told me, I really do think that he was the most loved child in the world. That's how he was made to feel.

yiddishkeit
/yid-ISH-kite/
n. Jewish way of life

Dad has told me this story many times of his Bubbie Elsie, whom I'm named after. She was *zaftig*, crass, larger than life, a loving woman. He would ride the bus with Bubbie Elsie and she would exclaim to everyone around her, "Look at my Shloimie, isn't he beautiful?" (Shloimie is his name in Yiddish, which she always called him.) My dad, the skinny little kid with snot running down his face, would always cringe in embarrassment.

zaftig
/zaff-tig/
adj. juicy; used to describe a woman or a girl who is plump. (Don't be mad at me, but it's only used to refer to a chubby or overweight woman, not a man.)

When he was seventeen, my dad had already met my mom and they were "going steady." He was in his last year of high school but couldn't take being so short of money, so he dropped out of regular high school, started to work full-time, and finished his high school diploma at night school.

For a few years, he continued to work during the day and pursue higher education at night. My parents married when they were both twenty-one years old, and two years later my dad earned his accounting degree from college, just when I was born. To build his career and provide for his growing family, Dad always had a very strong work ethic.

My dad also has a lighter side to his personality. He can be silly and funny, and he has LOTS of *mishegas.*

mishegas
/me-SHEH-gas/
n. craziness or insanity

Dad has a nickname for everyone. He can be really goofy at times. When we were little kids, he was always there to give me, my brothers, or my cousins his signature moves—the "claw," the "eye gouge"—or just to chase us around the house as we shrieked away.

And sometimes (OK, more than sometimes), he will say something that my mom and the rest of our family think is inappropriate. There are many times when something comes out of his mouth and we all just look at him with gaping mouths. In our family we've coined these moments as "Shirley-isms," after my Bubbie Shirley, who would say the most outlandish things. Although I consider myself to be politically correct, when my Bubbie Shirley or Dad would say something politically incorrect, I couldn't help laughing out loud. We all did. And then, of course, we admonished them about why they can't say what they said!

This is the dad I knew and grew up with at home. But as I got older, I realized there was another Stanley Udaskin too. One who showed up at work a lot different than how he showed up at home. And he would transform as soon as he left the house early in the morning dressed in his sharp suit and tie. When he'd come home late at night, the first thing he always did was change out of his suit and into more casual clothes, then pour himself a scotch. Then he would engage with us if we were still awake. We mostly saw our dad and played with him on the weekends.

When I started my first full-time job it was located in downtown Toronto, and I had moved back home to save money to pay off my student loans and all that fun stuff. Dad was working downtown as well, so we commuted together to work. This is how it went.

We would leave the house, both dressed in our business attire, and drive the fifteen minutes to the subway station in silence. After parking in the lot, we'd walk another five minutes to the subway and then find our seats. My dad would then open his newspaper (anyone remember actual newspapers?) and hand me a section to read. After a few minutes, we would switch sections and continue to read until our stops.

This was when I really understood why my mom, aunt, and uncle called my dad "Business Mode," or "BM" for short, when he would be direct or even curt at times at home when he was reading and one of us interrupted him with a question.

I guess I started to behave the same way, as my dad nicknamed me "Junior Business Mode" or "Junior BM."

ON MY OWN

Finally, I moved out of the house for good when I started a new job at Kraft Canada in marketing, in Midtown Toronto, and was on my own in more facets of my life than ever before. I started as a brand assistant, working my way through various roles in my career. I was mostly oblivious to how people at work perceived me, as I was too focused on getting my work done. A specific event at work was the beginning of my acknowledging how others reacted to me and perceived me at work.

Fifteen women were selected by my company to take part in a Women's Leadership workshop. We were all in marketing, at differing levels of the organization. Part of the exercises the facilitator took us through was getting feedback from one another. I was partnered up with a young woman named Vanessa, who was just one level below me at work.

Vanessa courageously told me that she used to be intimidated by me until she got to know me better. She said that she would often see me walk quickly and focused through the hallways of the office, describing it as zipping past everyone with a mission. She shared that she always thought I was unapproachable until she got to know me better and then realized that I was friendly, and, wow, she even liked me.

My reaction was "What? Me? Intimidating? What? Am I a *golem*? *Oy vey*."

golem
/GOH-lem/
n. a stupid and clumsy person, a blockhead

I guess I was in my "Business Mode."

Since then, sometimes I catch myself that my voice even changes when I'm at work. I could be working from home one day and I have my "work voice" on for conference calls, then switch it up totally without noticing into my "other Elisa voice" when talking with friends or my family.

This was the beginning of my journey to really try to listen to feedback from others and make changes as much as I could. No one likes 360-degree feedback or feedback from your manager or coworkers that is often packaged as "constructive criticism." Who likes to hear when they aren't doing a good job or not doing it in a good way?

I've realized that getting feedback is a gift. It really is. Managers would always tell me this and I would think that was just a standard line they used before they would launch into telling me something I had done wrong or needed to do better. I thought of it as criticism, instead of constructive criticism. But when I was open to feedback and then tried changing my approach and it magically had different and positive outcomes, I realized that it was a true gift. From then on I sought feedback from not only my managers, but also my peers, direct reports, and agency partners.

I personally try my darndest to be open to feedback and to change what I can—what I think is reasonable. After all, we are who we are and can't or shouldn't change completely. But when I get feedback, I realize that I really should think about it thoughtfully and carefully, and think about how I could do things differently.

WOULD IT KILL YOU TO STOP FOR A MINUTE OR TWO, SMILE, AND SAY HELLO?

I had a rude awakening when I started at Kraft. Up to this point in my life I had always spoken my mind, in classes and with friends and family. But at Kraft I was "coached" that there was a specific time and place for when my opinion would be welcomed, and in some cases should be held. For instance, in meetings with senior management and our advertising agency, when the agency was presenting new creative ideas to us, if I was allowed to be in the meeting it came with strict instructions to be quiet unless I was asked to speak (since I was at a junior level). So, I had to be on my toes. Sometimes the marketing director would want to take the lead on giving feedback to the agency, in which case I wasn't supposed to speak but was allowed in the meeting as a "learning experience."

Such a courtesy of them. So kind.

But other times, and I didn't get wind of this until right in the meeting, the creatives at the advertising agency would finish up their presentation and then the marketing director would turn to me and say, "Elisa, tell us what you think."

It was very unsettling to say the least.

Here is another thing that I found unsettling. I have always been an early riser and would get to work early, often one of the first few people in the office. Time and time again this same thing kept on happening. I would be sitting in my cubicle working away and my marketing director would pass by me on his way in toward his office. He always rang out, "Hey, how are you?" and kept on walking. He didn't wait for a reply, let alone look at me and smile. Off he went with my answer trailing behind him.

After quite a few times of this happening, it really bothered me. So the next morning as he passed by my cubicle, I tried to answer as fast as I could a rehearsed "Thank you for asking. I'm actually feeling quite bloated this morning. How are you?" But of course he was too quick for me and may have only heard the "Thank you for . . ." Or didn't hear me at all.

I worked away in this first role as brand assistant on the Philadelphia Cream Cheese brand, learning the ropes, the culture, and how we at Kraft worked together.

A year later I was promoted and shifted to work on another brand, Maxwell House. One day I was sitting in my cubicle, focused on my work, fixated on my computer, when I heard a voice.

"Hi, Elisa."

I looked up and saw my new marketing director, Dino Bianco, standing at the entrance of my cubicle. I immediately straightened up, took a pen in my hand with my notebook in the other, and said, "Hi, Dino."

He stood there and smiled.

"Is there something I can do for you?" I asked. "Is there a report you need me to pull?"

It became a bit awkward. He looked at me, smiled, and said, "Uh, no. I just came by to say hi."

Whoa. I almost fell off my swivel chair.

I didn't know what to do with this. I awkwardly blushed and then we talked for a couple of minutes.

As the weeks went by I learned in my new group that there are different kinds of managers. Managers and directors—they each have their own style. A company's culture is made up of the individuals. There will be all types of personalities and approaches. And I definitely liked *this one* better and would try to emulate Dino's approach for myself.

It may seem basic, but being a mensch, a good person to others, is so important. Sometimes we are too focused on projects, goals, and strategies, and we forget the basic human side of getting things done at work. We are often stressed or time-pressed and lose sight that it's not only what we do but also *how* we do it. How we show up every day to work. Basic manners like saying hello, please, and thank you. Giving a heartfelt greeting to your coworkers when you pass by them or enter a meeting room.

Being genuine is the key.

Work is so much more than deliverables, projects, or meetings. It is about our relationships with the people we see every day and spend most of our waking hours with. Over the years I have opened myself up, brought more of my whole self to work, which in turn has given me the gift of making terrific friends through work along the way.

BEING HUMAN AT WORK IS NOT A WEAKNESS

Here's a novel concept: you can be kind *and* do well at work, and succeed, get that promotion, climb the ladder, whatever you set your eyes on.

Yes, can you believe it?

It's true.

Other great books talk about why giving at work will make you more productive and successful. I want to talk about how being a mensch at work will make you a happier person (and yes, probably help you achieve your goals better/faster too!). The most important thing to remember is to be authentic.

Why do some people act like total schmucks at work? I know that everyone has their own baggage, so by no means can I answer this question perfectly, but here are some insights I've learned from people who have researched this subject.

Sometimes people think that if they show kindness they will appear weak.

However, I believe that showing your human side at work is actually the key to success. The best managers and leaders are the ones who are able to be human while still leading a team or a company. At the end of the day, your relationships are your most important assets at work.

Kindness is not a weakness. Building strong connections with people only increases your strength. Kindness does not replace the need to stick to timelines or run a successful business, but it changes how we approach achieving these goals.

It's not the "what" in these cases, it's the "how." You can still be in charge, lead the team, and act assertively. This is different from acting aggressively. Dare I say being a bully. In my experience I've respected and worked harder for managers who treated me well than those who weren't consistently nice all the time or who blew up when a mistake was made or a timeline wasn't met and they would berate our team.

Doesn't it feel good to like the people you work with and feel that they like you back? It sure helps those Monday blues when you look forward to going back to work after a lovely weekend.

Don't get me wrong. There are certainly going to be people at work whom you don't get along with, whom you clash with regularly. That's just life. But if you try to form a relationship with them, it will make it easier when you have these clashes and differences of opinion. If you get to know the other person a bit, you may even be able to muster up some empathy and deal with the situation better when they are acting in a rude way.

Last year I bumped into two former colleagues at a restaurant. While I was leading the category team as the marketer, both of these women were on the extended team, working in Research and Development. We had been in countless meetings, even on business trips together, and gotten to know one another personally through the years. I always enjoyed working with them.

I had left the company three years prior so I hadn't seen either of them in a long time. We were so excited to see one another. We immediately hugged with huge, warm smiles. The questions started popping all over the place. They asked about my kids. I asked one of them about her kids and the other how her mom was doing. We reminisced over funny stories about a business trip together in Switzerland.

It was such an awesome feeling. Did we talk about work projects? Recall when we launched a new variety of gum and how it was currently performing?

No, we didn't.

We talked about our personal lives. I realized that I knew a little about their lives, they knew about mine, and the relationships we had formed through work had been so much more than the work and projects themselves. It was the connections we had formed with one another that had made working together so rewarding.

You see, when you are at work, there are so many opportunities to get to know someone a little bit more, rather than just talking about the projects you are doing together. On a break at work, when you first get into the office, a few minutes before your shift or meeting starts, in the cafeteria. On a Monday you can just start with "How was your weekend?" and actually spend three minutes before a meeting starts to hear what everyone was up to that weekend.

But as we all know, it's not always warm and fuzzy with people at work. Inevitably there are going to be some situations that are really tough to get through, and especially to try to hold your sh*t and composure together and try your hardest to be a mensch.

When someone on your team or someone who works for you isn't pulling their weight, you could do a number of things. You could report them to your manager, *kvetch* about how they are slacking off or how they just don't get what they are supposed to do.

You could get frustrated with them directly and tell them that they suck.

Or you could be passive-aggressive and ignore them when they aren't pulling their weight, then say hi later like nothing is wrong.

I've done all of these things and been the subject of others doing them to me as well.

Relationships at work can be really tough. We all want to succeed, and yet at work our success is so interconnected with working with others.

One of the hardest things to do is to fire an employee when they aren't meeting expectations for their job. And all of the above reactions can come into play. But are these the only options? I don't think so. Let me tell you about a situation I was in and how it played out.

I had been promoted to a new role and inherited two direct reports in the new team. One of them, a really nice woman, was first introduced to me in a meeting along with human resources, as she was already on a PIP (performance improvement plan). This was a new experience for me.

Early on, we had a discussion about setting up a plan for her with goals, actions, and dates. We had regular check-ins scheduled together and with human resources. As the weeks went by, I grew to really like her a lot. She was great. But as much as she tried, her work wasn't meeting the standards. It just wasn't what we were looking for.

It was a tough situation.

The time came when we had her last check-in that would signal the start of her thirty-day final-notice period before she would be terminated. I felt sick to my stomach about having this discussion. In many ways I felt a lot of empathy for her, but in other ways she stressed me out because I had deliverables and she wasn't making it easy for me to get our team's work done.

I tried to think about the best way to approach this. How would I want to be treated in a similar situation?

I decided to be direct and honest with her. Through her tears and my nervousness, I told her that in these next thirty days it would be ideal if she took the time to think about what she really liked to do and start looking for another job. I would pick up her slack at work as much as I could. I still expected her to do her work, but I wanted to also give her space to figure out what was best for her. She could either really pick up the pace and turn herself around at our work, or focus her energies on figuring out her next steps.

The day came—the thirtieth day. I had met with the human resources director the day before, and she gave me all the paperwork I was to present to my direct report. My human resources counterpart was going to be at the meeting with me and we would go through it together.

However, before I could set up the meeting that morning, my direct report sent me a message asking if I could talk to her for a few minutes. We met in a closed office and she told me she was resigning. She had found a new job at a different company. She started to cry as she told me she knew she hadn't made things easy for me. I actually said, "Yes, you didn't." We had a chuckle and I told her how happy I was for her. I then went upstairs to my human resources counterpart, the termination paperwork in my hand, and told her that the situation was resolved.

And then I burst into tears. She asked me to sit down in her office and handed me a box of Kleenex. (You can always count on human resources people to have a box of Kleenex.) I apologized for crying and was embarrassed to be unprofessional. She was very kind and understanding, telling me that this situation was very stressful for me too, as I cared and that was a *good thing*.

Being human at work.

Crying at work.

I don't recommend doing it all the time (while I also don't recommend crying at home all the time). But when it happens and your emotions overcome you, it's OK.

It's really OK to show people at work that you feel, that you are human.

WAYS TO BE A MENSCH AT WORK

In Adam Grant's book *Give and Take*, he talks about why helping others drives our success at work. Rather than being focused solely on ourselves and how we can do a good job by working hard, we can recognize that our success is very dependent on our relationships and interactions with our colleagues. He argues that being generous and kind is the secret to getting ahead.

There really are easy ways to show kindness and respect in your everyday interactions at work that will, over time, become seamless, strengthen your relationships, build stronger teams, and, yes, make you happier too. If you are sincere and authentic it will be so powerful and you will be surprised that even though you give without expecting something in return, often your kindness will be reciprocated. That's just the way human nature works much of the time.

People can be givers or takers. *Mensches* or *schnorrers*.

> **schnorrer**
> /sh-NO-rer/
> *n.* a moocher, someone who wants to always get things for free; a parasite, someone who takes advantage of others

Wouldn't you want to be seen more as a mensch than a schnorrer at work?

I have been so fortunate to have had many people show kindness to me at work. In challenging situations, colleagues and partners helped me figure out a tough problem, "had my back" when I was proposing a controversial argument in a meeting, and, yes, were simply nice. Many of my former managers became friends and mentors long after we worked together. I know time can pass, and if I have a question or need advice, they are always there when I reach out to them.

What I've found about mentoring people is that it doesn't necessarily have to be only your direct reports or manager. People in other disciplines at your work, with different types of jobs, or even your suppliers or agency partners can be excellent mentees or mentors.

There is both formal and informal mentoring. It's about helping people get through tough situations at work. It could be that they are feeling totally overwhelmed with their workload and afraid to tell their manager. Or they can't figure out how to do something and are too embarrassed to ask their manager for fear of looking incompetent. Helping others succeed at work is the ultimate helper's high.

You will be faced with a multitude of situations at work where you have the opportunity to be kind, to support and help people. Some of these situations are not so obvious. But they can make a big impact on the other person.

Here's one personal example.

It seems to me that I am always the one that a presenter or speaker in a large meeting or presentation makes eye contact with and calls out for the first question. *Why is this?* I ask myself. *Because of my wild, curly hair?*

Probably not.

It's more likely because I always try my best to make eye contact with them and smile. It's tough being up in front of people, especially as many in the audience are multitasking on their phones. I've been in the situation many times when I was giving a presentation and looked out to the audience and saw some people busy on their phones, not paying attention to me at all or not even trying to hide the fact. So I have empathy for people when they are presenting in front of large groups. Regardless of their fancy high title in the organization, it's tough for everyone.

In fact, it can be pretty lonely for a senior person when people enter the room and take a seat as far away from them as they can. Although they may think they don't smell and are pretty sure they took a solid shower that morning, having people sit far away from you doesn't feel good at any level you are at. I try to give encouragement to any person presenting to a group. I make eye contact and smile as they speak. Perhaps I'll even sit up close near the speaker versus way in the back of the room.

Now that many of our meetings have transitioned to virtual versus in person, it's more important than ever to support your colleagues. How tough is it to be presenting virtually in a Zoom meeting or Google Hangout and you just know that most people are multitasking and only half listening to you? You pause in your presentation to ask the attendees a question and you literally hear crickets. Silence. Nothing. You feel like a total putz. It's awful. My hope is that you do your best to pay attention, support people during these virtual meetings, put yourself in their shoes, and behave like you would want others to when you are the one leading the meeting.

WHEN SOMEONE AT WORK IS GOING THROUGH A TOUGH PERSONAL TIME

Many of us have had a friend or acquaintance at work who was going through a tough time in their personal life, such as illness, divorce, or loss in their family. Perhaps it's someone you work with but are not close friends with, or it's the person you see every day working in the cafeteria. You hear from another coworker about this person's situation, usually said in a hushed, quiet voice so no one else can hear.

You want to do something for them but feel at a loss as to what would be appropriate. You may hesitate to do or say anything at all because you don't want to be intrusive and cross that line from "work friend" to "personal friend."

I would argue that this is an imaginary line. Relationships are relationships. And like I said earlier, we often spend more time with the people we work with than we do with our own families. We don't hesitate to wish someone at work a happy birthday. Everyone on the broader team will congregate for the surprise birthday cake that is rolled out. Who doesn't like a little break from work and a piece of cake? Even if we don't know the teammate well, we show up for the cake, say a quick happy birthday, and then go back to our work.

But when something happens that is so personal and sad, we will often be stuck in terms of what to do. When a friend is going through a rough time, our immediate impulse is to reach out and support them, even if we hesitate at first because we are uncomfortable. Why not bring this part of yourself to work as well? Get over any inhibitions about "crossing a personal line" and be kind and supportive.

There are many gestures you can make that aren't intrusive and respect their privacy. Here are a few ideas to consider:

- When you know someone is going through a hard time and you see them in a meeting or a public place, instead of just thinking about them, reach out to them in a private setting. Send a private message via email or text.
- Ask them to go for coffee or lunch, or a quick walk.
- Bring them their favorite coffee, drink, or treat you know they love.
- Offer to be a sounding board to listen to what they are going through.
- Ask them how they are managing to balance their workload with everything else that is going on.

And offer concrete ways you can help to lessen their burden.

• If a coworker has passed away, make a memorial donation in their honor. If someone close to your coworker has passed away, reach out to them to express your condolences.

The key is to be brave and reach out.

LOSING YOUR JOB

One of the most humbling things that can happen is losing your job. No matter what the circumstances are for you leaving, it's awful.

When I lost my job after close to twenty years at the same company, it was amazing how many people reached out to me to offer any help they could give, or even just to talk to me. And it was equally amazing to me how a few people whom I had worked with closely and become friends with at work (or so I thought) didn't reach out at all.

Really, was losing my job contagious?

Was I now a pariah?

That's how I felt sometimes.

It is very humbling to be looking for a job. Quite terrifying too. Your confidence can be at an all-time low. You are putting yourself out there constantly, waiting for rejection. You are so vulnerable.

This may also be the first time in your life that you are asking people outright to help you. Asking people for introductions in their networks, asking for a few minutes of their time in their busy schedules to speak with you.

So many unanswered emails and calls.

I know how this feels.

Three weeks after I lost my job, Adam and I went out with friends for dinner. One of the friends worked in the same industry as me, and over the years we had talked about our work travel—never crossing the line of getting into specifics, as our respective companies were competitors.

We started catching up about the kids, etc. Then I saw him take in a breath, and he blurted out, "Elisa, I wish I could help you, but you know my company will probably be going through changes and restructuring ourselves soon, so I really can't help you."

What? Did I even ask him for help?

No.

So why did he offer NOT to help me?

Weird.

It was unsettling and left me feeling totally yucky.

I replied that's OK, I understood. Even my husband, who usually doesn't notice these things, gave my knee a quick little squeeze under the table.

And our conversation moved on from there to other topics.

Our friend must have anticipated prior to our dinner that I would ask him to help me get a job at his company, which honestly was furthest from my mind. I didn't know much immediately after losing my job, but one thing I knew for sure was that I wanted to explore opportunities in a different industry altogether, maybe even make a complete career switch (which I did eventually).

Thankfully this was really the only major time I was disappointed in a friend when I lost my job. I received so much support from most people: former colleagues and managers, friends, and neighbors. And my family went above and beyond in terms of continuously checking in with me and showing me unconditional support.

My friend and neighbor Liz Szporn did the exact opposite of the friend at that awkward meal. I had only moved into the neighborhood six months prior to losing my job, so I really hadn't known Liz for very long. Liz was herself transitioning from a corporate career to being an entrepreneur and is one of the most generous people I know.

After a few months I decided that I was going to give this social entrepreneur thing a go. As I was building my social business, Caring Organizer, and launching my website and social media, money was very tight. I had to dig into my savings to fund my start-up. Liz selflessly shared the many tools she had used to launch her own online business a year prior and showed me how to use HubSpot, Mailchimp, and Canva, where I could economize, and how to develop amazing content and contacts on my own. She was a godsend.

One of the kindest things someone did for me was being honest and direct—even though it was uncomfortable.

Right after I lost my job, my friend Gregg Russo, who has a career as an executive-level human resources guy, offered to meet me for breakfast. He chose a Sunday morning at 8 a.m. at our local Panera. When we sat down at our table with our coffees, he looked at me and said, "Elisa, look what you're wearing."

I looked down at myself and saw no problem. I was wearing yoga pants and a sweatshirt, my hair was in a ponytail, and I had no makeup on. This was a Sunday morning with a friend for breakfast, no?

He proceeded to tell me that he knew how I felt (sad, maybe even a bit depressed), but that I had to get dressed in the morning like I was going to work. He conceded I could dress business casual, but I must get dressed and not look like a *shmatta* every day. I told him I just didn't have the *koyach* to get dressed up every day. We negotiated and I said I would try to do it three days a week to start.

shmatta

/shm-A-tah/

n. a rag, old piece of clothing

koyach

/koy-AKH/

n. inner strength, energy, wherewithal

To be honest, it was embarrassing when he pointed out how I looked. I never would have shown up to work that way, ever. I appreciated his direct and honest feedback and that he cared enough to tell me what he knew I needed to hear. Sometimes being kind is also giving difficult news—straight talk.

Sometimes it's only after you've experienced something yourself that you truly can put yourself in another person's shoes. Now that I've gone through this, I try my best to be extra supportive of others, to accept requests to talk about advice and networking, and to just be an open ear and listen.

I truly believe that everyone can take ten minutes to help out someone else. It's only ten minutes in your entire life.

CHAPTER SEVEN

Time to Really Be a Mensch: Death

Oy, I'm not going to lie to you. This is a tough one. It's uncomfortable, scary, messy. It can bring out the best in us and, yes, the worst in us. We can rise to the occasion and be a super mensch, or we can hide under our blanket, hoping that it will just go away.

Death.

When someone we care about passes away or someone we know loses a loved one, what do we do? What do we say?

Do we run over to their house immediately? Or give them space? Or do nothing at all?

I find this one to be so difficult at times. Even if it's one of my best friends, I'm not sure what to do in that moment after I hear that someone close to them has passed away.

What I've come to realize is that these are some of the most important times to dig deep into yourself and muster all your courage to reach out and support someone. It's tough, really tough. Fraught with emotions.

Say it's a friend whom you see every month for dinner. It's easy to reach out to make plans for your next dinner, but when they are going through something tough, sometimes we get stuck. We hesitate to reach out. Sometimes, if I may be so direct, we treat them like they have the plague. We treat them differently.

DEATH REALLY SUCKS

The first funeral I went to without my parents by my side was for my high school friend Kathy's dad, when I was nineteen. It has stuck with me ever since because of how scared and uncomfortable I was. It was a Greek Orthodox funeral, and while I had been to many happy Greek festivals and gatherings, I had never been to a Greek Orthodox funeral and didn't know what to expect.

Inside the church I saw that people were waiting in line to walk toward where my friend's father lay in an open casket. As I got closer, I noticed people were crossing themselves over the casket and I started to panic. Was I supposed to cross myself too? This wasn't my religion, but I wanted to do the right thing and be respectful.

As I approached the casket, the strong smell of incense overwhelmed me. I had never seen a dead body in person up to this point. I solemnly bowed my head, said a prayer in my head for my friend's father, and then proceeded to follow the line in front of me back down the church aisle.

Attending a funeral is very stressful. If it's uncomfortable for most of us adults, can you imagine what it's like for teenagers and kids?

But sometimes we can learn so much from the kids. Once in a while they surprise us. Such was the case when a death touched my son's hockey team.

We heard the sad news that the father of one of my son's hockey teammates had died. Then we received an email from the Booster Club president with the details of the service and the request that all the boys who were in town (it was early summer) please attend the visitation together and wear their black hockey jerseys.

What happened next got me all verklempt and brought me to tears.

I drove my son to the visitation. We parked in the parking lot and got out of the car, and I started walking toward the building where the visitation was taking place. Then I noticed that Kobi wasn't following me. I turned around and asked why he wasn't coming, and he told me that the captains of the hockey team had sent around a message to all the players to meet together in the parking lot, where they would get their jerseys and go in together.

I went in first and greeted the mourning mom and her kids as I approached my turn in line. When I spoke with the mom, I told her that the hockey team players were all coming to pay their respects. She said that her son was really hoping they would come, and she was so pleased to hear they were going to be there for him.

After my turn greeting the family, I stepped aside and waited near the other people who were standing around. Then I saw the boys (ranging in age from fourteen to eighteen) file in solemnly, wearing their black hockey jerseys over dress shirts with ties. Remember, it was summer and very hot out.

The boys quietly queued up in the visitor line. When the boy who had lost his dad saw them, he walked over, and one by one made his way down the line, each boy hugging him tightly.

The boys stayed in the line and continued to walk with it and then greeted the other family members.

I became totally verklempt. I was so overcome with emotion about how amazing and brave these teenagers were—usually yelling smack to one another in the locker room—and how they just knew how to act in this uncomfortable situation and give comfort to their teammate and his family. I was so proud of them and also had great respect for their parents for raising such amazing kids.

EXCUSES, EXCUSES

Who likes to feel uncomfortable? I sure don't. I would prefer to ignore uncomfortable situations and conversations. I would much rather pretend they aren't happening and hope that maybe they will go away.

Death is certainly at the top of the list, or close to the top, of uncomfortable situations. It is uncomfortable for all of us, which is the reason why we sometimes back away from it and hesitate to reach out when it enters our lives. When friends or family lose a loved one, we sometimes find ourselves making excuses and justifying this by saying that the grieving person needs space and does not need us. We don't know what to say or what to do. We don't want to bother them.

We all have excuses for why we don't do things immediately, or why we don't do them at all. Sometimes we say them aloud to someone else, and other times we say them to ourselves in our heads. This is normal. Don't beat yourself up.

But remember, you're a mensch. Try to acknowledge why you are making excuses, and face them head-on. You will probably find a way that is more comfortable for you to do something.

Don't let your inner voice convince you that you shouldn't reach out. In these cases, it is just the opposite. Seriously, I have little patience for excuses. I learned through the years that if I have a problem, instead of just kvetching about it, it's best to kvetch *and* have suggestions, ideas, or alternatives for how to solve or address it. No one wants to hear a kvetch. And I'm sure you don't even like hearing yourself kvetch as well.

The most important thing to do is to accept that you are in an uncomfortable place and become comfortable in the discomfort. Ultimately, it is about putting yourself out there. And mostly recognizing that this is not about you, it is about the person you care about.

You Don't Have Time

Time is a very easy excuse when it comes to things you are uncomfortable with. Death is uncomfortable for all of us. We may say, "I'm so busy with work, I didn't have time to go to the funeral." Or "I wish I had the time to go to the shiva or visitation, but you know how busy I am after work, running around with the kids, making dinner, so much to do."

Oy, abrocht. For goodness' sake—you DO have the time.

It doesn't take so long to do something to express your condolences. Think about how much time you spend every day on your phone checking social media and the news and playing online games. Yeah, you have the time for this.

Time isn't the obstacle; it's stepping into the uncomfortable that's preventing you from reaching out. Once you realize this, you can try to overcome the reasons behind your hesitation, and it will be easier for you to reach out. And there are so many really easy things you can do to support people, which I will get into shortly. Things that don't take too much time. The key is to act on it when you hear about the person or family that needs your support.

What in the World Should You Say?

"I don't know what to say."
"I have no words."
"I'm serious, I am getting fully anxious now. I really have no idea what to say."
"It's stressing me out so much. I'm just not going to call her."
"She'll understand."
"I hope she understands."

I know I've had these thoughts many, many times. I hesitate to pay a condolence visit or reach out to a friend because I get anxious that I don't know what to say to them. Their loss is so profound to them, in my mind there is nothing I can say that will ease their pain.

Or worse, I fear I'll say the wrong thing. Believe me, I've said "the wrong thing" many times. I just hope that my intentions were accepted in a good way and the person was kind enough to understand that I fumbled over my words because I was so uncomfortable.

I don't want it to be a trivial or cliché-sounding "I'm sorry for your loss." But if I do start with that phrase to help me get started, what do I say after that?

Although many people see me as an assertive ballbuster, I can get very emotional too. There have been times that frankly I worry I won't be able to hold my sh*t together. I don't want to break down and cry to the person—a family member, friend, or acquaintance—when I call them or see them after they've experienced a loss. I want to be strong. And yes, to hold my sh*t together for them, and for myself.

Sometimes if the death is so shocking, like a sudden death of a spouse or child, I feel uncomfortable approaching people. It is because I think I need to be strong and hold it together for them and I don't want to break down and cause them to break down. (Leona L.)

I remember the time when my friend's brother passed away years ago. He had already had two kidney transplants over the past few years. I was at a conference in Washington, D.C., when I received her text that her brother had died. I found a quiet, private place in the conference center's coat closet and called her. I took a deep breath, determined to hold it together and be strong for her, as I dialed her number. When I heard her voice and she started to talk about the last moments with her brother, I just started to cry. And we cried together. It was OK, I realized. I continued to sob quietly as she cried and talked. I was there for her, sharing in her grief.

HERE ARE SOME MENSCH THINGS YOU CAN SAY

- Talk about the person who passed away. Don't avoid doing this, although you may be uncomfortable at first. Use their name. Let your friend know that you think about their loved one and have not forgotten about them.
- Remember that you can't take away their pain, so the most important thing you can do is make them feel understood and loved. Say something like: "While there is nothing I can do to change things, I want you to know that I am here for you and you have my love and support." This shows them that there is meaning behind your words

instead of some of the clichés that we typically
rely on.

- Don't ask what you can do to help. Be proactive and
be prepared to offer something specific. For example: "I am going to the grocery store. Please give
me your list and I'll pick up your groceries too." Or
"I would like to bring you dinner this week." Or "I
can drive your child to practice this week."

- The most important thing you can do for a grieving person is to stand with them, not apart from
them. It can be uncomfortable, but it is the truest
form of kindness we can express through both
our words and actions.

- Sometimes, though, it is not about saying anything.
It is about giving them a hug or holding their hand.
It is about having the ability to sit with them in
silence or just listen. That too can be uncomfortable but sometimes it is just what they need.

Stop and Just Listen

For goodness' sake, don't be a *yenta*.

> **yenta**
> /YEN-ta/
> *n.* a gossip or busybody

Have you ever been in a conversation like this one? Perhaps
not the same situation exactly, but you'll get the idea.

YOU: My godson has cancer. I'm so upset. He's an
amazing young man and the doctors say that
with treatment he has a chance of beating it.

FRIEND: Oh. You know, my neighbor's nephew had the same thing. They tried everything, but it didn't work in the end. He DIED. So sad.

I do this all the time. Or I used to. When someone would tell me about someone they cared about who died or was sick, I would immediately start talking about someone else I knew going through a similar thing.

After I finished my long story, I would say, "Hello? Are you still there?" Because most often I would be met with silence on the other end of the phone.

Why?

I started to realize it was because I wasn't really listening to them. I turned the conversation away from them to something else entirely. Once I acknowledged I was doing this a lot, I tried to stop. But I do slip into doing it sometimes. After all, I'm only human, right?

Sometimes when a friend is sharing a personal story with us that is very emotional—their feelings about how sad, or hurt, or stressed out they are—we tend to reply with stories of our own that are similar. And we fall down that rabbit hole of starting to kvetch about our own *tsuris*. Or someone's else's *tsuris* . . . instead of addressing what our friend is sharing with us. But that's not what they need. They just need to be heard.

tsuris
/TSORE-iss/
n. troubles and worries; problems

Why do we do this? We may get caught up in worrying about not saying the right thing, so we talk about something else. We don't want people to feel alone, but to know that there are others who have gone through the same thing. Or we get uncomfortable when our friend is sharing their emotions so openly, and so our default is to go into a more comfortable space for ourselves, not addressing or replying directly to their emotions.

The result is we unintentionally draw the focus away from our friend and onto ourselves, leaving our friend feeling unheard, and maybe even a little worse after talking with us.

The next time someone is sharing their feelings of a difficult situation they are going through, try these suggestions:

- Listen intently and don't interrupt with your own story.
- Keep your replies focused on what the person is sharing with you.
- Ask questions to encourage the person to continue.
- Make a conscious effort to listen more and talk less.
- After the person has shared with you, ask them if they'd like advice or if they just want you to listen. You may find that they actually DO want advice and then go for it! But then, they may just need to talk to you and have you listen.

Most important, try not to be too nervous or worried about what you say. If you try these suggestions, you actually will be saying less and listening more.

But You Live Far Away

As an adult, I have moved with my family from Toronto, Canada, to New Jersey, to Singapore, and then back to New Jersey. These experiences have been amazing for me and my family. I've been fortunate to have been able to maintain close relationships with family and friends in Toronto, my "roots." I've been lucky to make new friends in New Jersey and then again in Singapore. Friends who were like family. Close relationships that will last a lifetime.

There have been many times when I've been living in one country and heard that someone I care about is ill or has passed away and I've been very far away. It's a terrible feeling to not be able to grab my keys, jump in the car, and head over to see them. I've felt at a loss many, many times—and learned along the way how to still reach out and support them while not being there physically.

Today's world is a spread-out one. It is far more common that we will live in a separate city from our children, family, and lifelong friends. And there are times when we cannot travel to be with them, as during COVID-19, with so many travel restrictions and cautions not to see people in person, especially the elderly, who are most vulnerable to getting sick. Phone calls, occasional visits, and social media make it easier for us to stay connected to our community of people, but what happens when there is a death or illness that requires a more meaningful connection? With the absence of your physical presence, what tangible things can you do to ensure that you are being supportive to a loved one or friend?

For starters, it is really important to know that you can absolutely be there for someone you care about when they are going through a difficult time, even in the absence of your physical presence. Relinquish the feeling of being paralyzed by your physical distance and shift your focus to the positive. Spend time thinking about what you can do in this situation, rather than what is not possible.

At my mother's funeral, I looked into the crowd to see a friend who drove over an hour and half to be there. (I didn't know she was coming.) Friends

from afar sent meals, which were unexpected,
and I appreciated knowing we were being thought
of. (Jessica C.)

MENSCH THINGS YOU CAN DO (FROM ANYWHERE)

- Send a donation in memory of the person who passed away. Look up the obituary on either the funeral home website or the local newspaper online. If you don't have the information for where to send a donation and don't want to ask the grieving person, simply google the name of the person who passed away and their city, and typically the search will serve up the obituary details that have the family's request for memorial donations to their charity of choice.
- When someone has passed away, send the family a meal. Find a local restaurant that delivers and send them dinner.
- Send a condolence message. Email, text, and private messaging through social media are immediate ways to communicate. But follow up with a physical card that is more meaningful and creates a personal connection. Let them know you are thinking of them and share a memory you have.

You Haven't Been in Touch in Years

Over the years I've lost touch with some friends. It was especially hard to keep in touch with everyone as I moved a few times and grew up before there was Facebook, texting, etc.

I can still remember some childhood friends' parents' home phone numbers by heart, yet I haven't stayed in touch. Such is the way life goes.

People from my distant past reached out to me when my mom passed away and I felt so pleased that they were thinking of me, but much more that they were thinking of my mom. (Lauren W.)

A couple of years ago I heard through the grapevine that my really good friend from middle school in Ottawa had a family crisis involving her father. It took me back to memories of times spent with her family and remembering how kind her parents were to me whenever I was at their house. I really liked her a lot, but we grew up in different directions.

It was an awkward situation that they were going through, so I wasn't sure if I should reach out. I didn't want to be nosy, have it seem like I was being a yenta by calling her after all these years. I decided that email was probably best. I tracked down her email address from someone I was still in touch with in Ottawa.

I simply emailed "I heard about your dad and wanted you to know that I'm thinking of you."

I didn't expect an answer. I knew she and her family must be extremely overwhelmed. However, she emailed me right back with "When the news came out about my dad, I thought back to my friends growing up, including you, and that you may have heard what was going on and you knew my dad." She said that "reaching out to her was like a warm blanket enveloping her with love."

Since then we have stayed in touch. Not very frequently. She's not on Facebook, which I find to be an awesome way to keep in touch with people. But now she is back at the forefront of my heart and mind and I think of her more often.

As we go through our lives, we are naturally close to people at certain times, then we may lose touch. School, our neighbors from when we were growing up, university, different jobs.
We grow, move, have new experiences, and sometimes drift
away from these people we were once so close with and inter-
acted with daily at that time. We haven't lost our fondness for
them; life just keeps on moving along, taking us in different
directions.

These connections never go away. The strong bonds you
formed at the time, maybe even years ago, have created lasting
memories. When you hear that someone you have lost touch
with is going through a really rough time, reaching out to them
will bring a ray of sunshine into their dark days. Especially since
it is unexpected. When they see your text, hear your voice, or
see you at the funeral or visitation, it will conjure up warm and
happy feelings and make them feel so supported and loved.

> *A childhood friend whose family was very close
> to ours for many years and then lost touch sent
> an email when she heard my dad had died. She
> also came to his shiva. It made me realize that
> the strong bond we once had as kids had a solid
> foundation, and I realized support can come
> from outside your closest circle. We have since
> remained infrequently in touch, and when her
> mother died a few months ago, I sent her an email
> with some memories of her mom, which she said
> meant a lot. (Sherry D.)*

They Really Are Your Friend's Friend, Not Yours

Acquaintances. This can be a bit tricky. You hear from your
friend about their friend who is going through a really tough

time—perhaps a death in their family or a serious illness. You see this person only when you are with your friend, at the book club get-together, or at a large birthday party. You like them a lot and when you see them you always have a good time together.

But are they really *your* friend?

This is when the inner evaluation starts happening. You aren't *really* close friends yourselves. Is it too weird if you do something to reach out? Would they find it weird?

> *If it is an acquaintance and not a close friend, I will reach out via email or text rather than by phone. I will offer help in the means of running errands, dropping off food, helping out with their kids, whatever they need or want. I just let them know I am there for them and ask them to take me up on my offer. I will follow up if they don't and continue to offer help. (Robyn F.)*

I really believe you can't go wrong here. There's only upside versus not doing anything at all. By reaching out to them, you will be giving them an even warmer blanket of love to surround them with. (I'm really into this warm blanket of love analogy.)

Let me share a story of when I experienced this situation myself.

A few years ago a friend of a friend in my community had a brain aneurysm. She was a teacher at a local high school and on the first day of school she collapsed and then was in the hospital for many weeks. She was going to have a very long recovery, and her husband and three kids would need a lot of support. I definitely had met her and her husband before, but by no means did we have a close relationship.

However, when I heard what her family was going through it really touched me. My friend told me that a meal schedule was being circulated, and so I signed up for a few weeks down the line to make dinner for them. I was a bit worried that the husband wouldn't recognize my name on the meal schedule, and it would be very strange for him to receive a meal from me. I told my friend my worry and she told me that they needed as much support as they could get and I should do it.

There was no need for an acknowledgment from the family. I just felt compelled to do something to help them out. I didn't reach out in any other way, as in this situation I thought it best to do something on the periphery. I made a dinner of chicken schnitzel, roasted potatoes, and salad (one of my standard meals), packed it up, and dropped it off at their house in the cooler that was left on the back deck for people to leave their food in.

We all have so many acquaintances that we may not even realize just how big our "village" is. People you know and see frequently at your kids' activities or sports, at your friend's annual barbecue or Christmas party. When you see them you make small talk.

But are they really *your* "friends"? Hmm . . . now the definition of friends and evaluating it comes in. Perhaps you don't talk on the phone or go out and socialize together, but you definitely have a relationship with them. You probably even see them more often than your "friends" during peak season of a sport or activity.

I know this is the case for me and hockey parents. During hockey season (which sometimes doesn't seem to ever end!), we see the same parents a couple of times a week. We sit together in the stands, and we chat before and after the games as we wait for our kids to get on the ice or change after a game. Lots of small talk, but we do get to know one another. And we *do* have a relationship. I literally don't socialize with my other friends during hockey season. They know that. Maybe they don't like it. But we are so busy with hockey games and tournaments on the weekends that it's just the way we fly.

For one of my son's hockey teams I would sit with one mom at almost every game. A couple of months after the season ended, I received a group email from our Booster Club president that this woman's husband had passed away from cancer. I was totally shocked. Didn't I just sit with his wife once a week for multiple weeks and chat? She never once said anything about her husband being sick.

I went to the visitation for her husband and when it was my turn to greet her, she spoke first and said to me, "I know you didn't know about how sick my husband was. I just didn't want to talk about it when we were at hockey. I knew you would be surprised." We hugged and I told her that I would love to get together for coffee when she was ready. Up to that point, we never got together outside of hockey. She said she would really enjoy that.

After a couple of weeks I reached out to her and we did go for coffee. We talked about her husband, how she was doing, how her kids were doing. She gave me the best compliment when she told me that many people had asked to see her and she was hesitant about many of them, but she knew that she would enjoy my company and she did! Wow, that sure felt good.

Sometimes when you are not close, you want to make sure you are not overstepping your relationship—so you have to find ways to show how much you care, without getting yourself in the middle of their mourning. (Lisa S.)

There is nothing more unexpected and appreciated than a kind and genuine note/email from a friend or even acquaintance, just saying that they are thinking of you and please reach out if there is anything you need. This happened over and over when my father passed away. Also, notes from people after he passed, telling me stories (some I hadn't heard), were a pure form of therapy. I still have them and read them on occasion (twenty years later). (Heather S.)

SHOW UP!

Depending on the situation, attend the funeral or visitation or shiva. If you can't be there in person, show up in another way. BE THERE for them figuratively.

The key is being proactive by anticipating the grieving person's needs. It requires you to think about subtle ways in which you can let them know that you are thinking about them and their needs and are there to support them. These ideas range from small to large, but their impact will be the same.

It is important not to pose the general question "What can I do for you?" They will naturally say there is nothing they need. Instead, make suggestions. It can be a small gesture or a larger one: buying them a coffee, picking up their kids from an activity, doing an errand, sending a meal that can be frozen and reheated for when they need it, taking out the garbage. Be specific in your offers. Don't make them have to think of what they need help with.

> *When people ask open-ended questions like "What can I do?" or "Let me know what you need," I find that I tend not to have a reply. I have enough going on. I just want people to do things (or not) but not to make it up to me to come up with a list or a task for them. (Sherry D.)*

MENSCH THINGS YOU CAN DO

- Send them a handwritten sympathy card. In it share a memory you have of the person who passed, or if you didn't know the person, then simply let them know you are thinking of them.
- Cooking will be the last thing on their mind. Make them dinner and drop it off at their house.
- Give them a restaurant gift card to one of their favorite restaurants.
- Be creative and make your own vouchers for household chores that they can remit at any time. For example, taking out their garbage or recycling.
- Hire a cleaning service to come to their home after the first week of mourning when they've had many people at their home and a couple of times after as well.
- Set up a neighborhood schedule to shovel the driveway or mow the lawn.
- Purchase a gift card for a massage or pedicure. Taking a moment for themselves will be hard at first. But as time goes by, and the initial influx of visitors starts to lessen, they will find comfort in something that helps them relax. Help them along with a gift card to a spa.

BE THE GUIDE WHEN PEOPLE ARE FISH OUT OF WATER

There are often times when we want to pay our respects to a friend, a neighbor, or a coworker who has suffered a loss in their family, but we may not be familiar with their customs and thus feel uncomfortable in how to show our support. While traditions in mourning vary by culture, one thing is a near guarantee. Showing love and support is universal.

In these situations, reach out to someone you know who shares their traditions and ask them for advice on what to do. You can also use "the google"! The internet has a wealth of information and will give you some general guidelines on mourning practices for different cultures and religions.

Likewise, if you are attending a funeral, visitation, or shiva for someone where you know the customs, why not help others who aren't as familiar and perhaps look uncomfortable? You can be the gentle guide to help them with their discomfort so they can show their support. It's often not very hard to identify these people at the funeral or visitation. They look very uncomfortable and generally are fidgeting. Approach carefully. But do approach! Nothing bad will happen to you but a lot of good could come out of it by helping someone else out of their discomfort.

Oy, do I have stories to share with you about this.

When my father-in-law passed away, we sat shiva at my sister-in-law's house. I was busy organizing the food and making sure that the mourners were comfortable. At one point when the house was full of visitors, I walked into the kitchen and saw a small group of people standing together and looking uncomfortable. I immediately surmised that they must be colleagues of my sister-in-law's from work. I went over to introduce myself, and yup, I was right. I realized that they weren't sure what to do at a shiva house and were thus very uncomfortable. I told them how kind it was for them to come pay their respects and that they could go into the living room where my sister-in-law was sitting and speak with her. I helped to guide them through their discomfort.

My mom told me the story of a funeral she went to of a family friend of ours. They were at the cemetery and after the prayers the tradition was for people to take turns shoveling earth into the open grave to cover the coffin.

My mom noticed a small group of men right beside her, who she guessed were friends of the son's. They stood watching. My mom quietly asked them if they knew what was happening and why people were shoveling in the earth. They replied that they didn't know and weren't familiar with this. She explained that in Jewish tradition it is customary for people to show their respects by taking turns shoveling earth over the coffin until it is completely covered. And then she suggested to them that if they wanted to show respect for their friend's mom, how to do it.

The three men then walked up to the grave in the small queue and took their turns shoveling in the earth to pay their respects to their friend's mom. They then walked back to where they had been standing with my mom and thanked her for helping them. They felt better that they didn't just stand there, but actively did something that they knew was important to their friend.

One last story to share. About ten years ago my friend's father passed away suddenly. It was tragic. Many of her friends, including myself, mobilized immediately to travel to the funeral, which was in another city from where we each lived.

When I got to the chapel, my friend was standing inside at the front. I went up and gave her a big hug as we both cried. More and more people started to file in and her other friends began to arrive.

A few of them walked toward her and were stopped by one of her mom's friends, who told them not to go over to her, she didn't want it. They came back to sit in the pew beside me and were embarrassed that they had made that overture, fearing they had done something wrong.

My friend was now standing alone up front with her sister and mom off a bit to the side, talking with other people, and I knew that we still had a few minutes before the service was to begin. So I gathered her friends and said, "Follow me and don't worry about that lady." I literally shielded them as we walked up to the front together, and I gave them space to hug our friend. It took a total of three minutes and I knew it comforted my friend greatly.

This is a case when you need to read a situation, think on your feet, and then do what you think is best. So long as you are always polite, you usually will do the "right thing."

BRING PEOPLE TOGETHER

As you may have guessed by now, I am an organizer type of person. There is nothing I love more than bringing out that Excel sheet and organizing anything from a large dinner party to a volunteer initiative that I'm leading.

Some of us are natural organizers, while others aren't as comfortable taking the lead, but are more than willing and happy to participate when someone else does the organizing. We need both types of people, that's for sure. I would never ever have a successful volunteer program if I didn't have people sign up to do the actual volunteering.

When someone you know experiences a death in the family, maybe you're the person who gets organized to rally support from all their other friends, family, and community. This is where there are some areas that are obvious in terms of what they need (e.g., meals), and others that aren't as comfortable to talk about.

When someone has lost a loved one, they are often inundated immediately afterward with people dropping off food. But as time goes on, it dwindles off and they may still be needing the meal support. This will depend on their situation, so it is good to check in to see what they need.

You could organize a meal schedule for them. So as not to be too overwhelming, perhaps schedule for three dinners to be sent a week. Specify a drop-off time frame and a place outside their house where a cooler can be kept to receive meals while respecting their privacy.

You really never know what people are going through. My bubbie always said, "You aren't living under their bed; you don't know what is happening in their home." Your friend may have a big house and go on vacations, and you think, *Oh, they will be fine financially*. However, this friend may be over their head in financial obligations. With perhaps medical bills, funeral bills, and the loss of a key family member's income, they are having a tough time making ends meet or worrying that they will in the near future.

No one can assume people are OK financially because we don't know people's private situations. We tend to be more comfortable asking, "How are you doing?" Maybe "how are you feeling?" But much less so about inquiring how they are coping from a financial perspective. It's very taboo in our society to speak about our finances with one another, and we don't want to seem like we are being nosy.

One suggestion is to have a gentle, candid conversation with your friend and offer to set up a GoFundMe for them. Let them know that people want to help and aren't judging. Others just really want to help in the best way the bereaved family needs to be supported. The fundraiser could be to cover medical and funeral bills, or it could be something like setting up a college fund for the children left behind.

I struggle with knowing how much to reach out during other people's crises. I want to be there for them, but I don't want to bother them or make them feel like they have to respond when I call or text. I also want to respect people's privacy.

Everyone handles crises differently. My illness was quite public, but some people wish to deal with their own situations privately. My meal schedule was perfect—whenever someone asked how they could help, I just gave them my friend's email so that they could be added to the meal schedule. People could sign up to cook if they wanted or send a gift card. It kept people informed and gave people a great opportunity to help out. I am always worried about bothering people who are not good friends. I like the idea of a contact person who can relay info about how someone is doing/what they need. It just takes one person to take the reins. (Cathleen M.)

LASTLY, GRIEF IS NEVER REALLY "OVER"

I've seen from my friends and family who have lost a parent that their grief never really ends. They think about their mom or dad constantly. They talk about them in speeches at celebrations, saying that they really miss them. Sometimes they will post memories on Facebook on their parent's birthday or the anniversary of when they passed away. But that's only what we on social media see. What really goes on is that they miss that person every single day. In their book *Option B: Facing Adversity, Building Resilience, and Finding Joy*, authors Sheryl Sandberg and Adam Grant say, "Grief doesn't share its schedule with anyone; we all grieve differently and in our own time."[9]

When someone has experienced a profound loss, often the really hard times begin for them after the initial mourning

9. *Option B: Facing Adversity, Building Resilience, and Finding Joy*, by Sheryl Sandberg and Adam Grant. Knopf, 2017.

period. The influx of messages and calls and the wave of people through their house are gone and there aren't as many distractions. It can be lonely and the loss of their loved one that much more apparent, which is why showing your ongoing support after the first few days is just as important, if not more so. Grief doesn't have a time limit.

Immediately following a loss, people are often supported for a few days or weeks, but then people stop calling or coming by. This leaves people feeling isolated and depressed, and usually the last thing they're going to do is call you for anything.

As a mensch, here are some proactive things you can do to help your friend or family member:

- Make room at your table. Invite them over for dinner regularly. Or send them dinner if that's a better option.
- Set a regular time that you will connect with them, either by phone or in person. This will be something they can look forward to that will be in their calendar as a regular occurrence.
- Continue to stay in touch via text, email, or phone calls. A simple "I'm thinking of you today" can do wonders. Don't get insulted if your messages aren't returned right away. The person will see and feel that they are loved; they may just not be ready to communicate that day. Keep trying, while not being overbearing.
- Try to tackle a project with them, such as cleaning up the house or going through old clothes. Whatever project they need to take care of, offer to do it with them.
- Send flowers or even a small treat on a regular basis. Just because you are thinking of them. It's something to brighten their day.

- If they have kids, offer to babysit to give them a break.

- Depending on their situation, for instance if they are very overwhelmed, a widow or widower who is elderly, or one who has young children, you may want to continue to send them meals and organize a rotation with their friends and neighbors.

- And in cases where you have not had a chance to initially visit, remember it is never too late to show your support. It is natural to be hesitant to reach out if you think too much time has passed and it's now awkward. A different way to think about it, though, is that for the mourner, your reaching out may be even more meaningful since the initial wave of visitors is gone and they may be feeling alone.

When my mother-in-law passed in 2017, one of the people on my team sent a sympathy card to my husband and me, and every year on the anniversary of my mother-in-law's death sends a lovely email to me. It touches me that she takes the time to send the note and that she cares. (Terrie-Lynne D.)

Death is very uncomfortable. I know it is really hard to reach out to someone when they are grieving, but I also know that you can do it. You have it in you to muster up your courage, be brave, reach out, and show your love and support.

CHAPTER EIGHT

Time to Really Be a Mensch: Illness

"Did you hear that she has . . . (whispers) *cancer*?"

Why is it that when we tell someone about another person who is sick, we always say the sickness part in a low, almost whispery voice? Like it's a secret, or something to be ashamed about. I know I do it myself, without meaning to. And you probably do it too. Maybe it's because we've heard it being said this way in many TV and movie scenes for dramatic effect. Or because that's how we've heard other people say it to each other in real life.

We like to hear about other people and what they're going through; it's just the way it is. We are inherently curious beings.

And yes, we're sometimes just nosy.

Then the grapevine starts. The person we tell (after we, of course, tell them *not* to tell anyone else) tells another and then another. And it goes on.

There *is* an upside to this grapevine. Hopefully the more people who know, the more people will offer and give support to the person who is ill and their family.

When I hear that someone is ill, I am often confused over what to do about it, and sometimes I second-guess my initial instinct to reach out. I think, *I don't want to intrude or bother them.* Perhaps they are an acquaintance and I think, *They have other people to support them; they don't really need me.*

When someone passes away, I can go to the funeral or visitation. That's the most straightforward thing to do. These built-in customs let me know how I can pay my respects. But when someone is sick, there is no road map of what to do. It so depends on the situation and could even change week by week. The person may not be up for a visit, so overwhelmed with being ill and all the other responsibilities they have to juggle.

It's tricky.

When someone's ill, I get nervous. I don't know what to do and sometimes I procrastinate to reach out because I'm uncomfortable.

But if we acknowledge that it's our fear or discomfort that is preventing us to reach out, then we can be compassionate with ourselves. Stop beating ourselves up, feeling guilty or ashamed that we haven't done anything. Sit in the uncomfortable for a while. Then think of what's best for us. Can we overcome our fear and visit in person? Maybe not. And that's OK. We can do other things that we find more comfortable. The important thing is to do *something*, or we will be ridden with guilt. Be kind to ourselves.

As I've tried to convey in this book, my strong belief is that *this is the time* to reach out and be there for them. But be aware and respectful of what we do and what we say (as much as we can). Whenever I've overcome my hesitation, even fear, of reaching out (no one likes to do the wrong thing, or feel rebuffed in any way), it is always met with the same response—gratitude. Especially when it's someone who wasn't expecting to hear from me.

Here's a little story I'd like to share.

I have a neighbor, Anne, who lives two houses away from me. I used to see her most mornings from my kitchen window, walking to the bus stop with her two young kids, when I was making my coffee or cleaning up the kitchen mess from the night before. Last year, I heard through another neighbor who is close friends with her that Anne's brother had a serious brain injury and was in intensive care at the hospital. Anne was juggling visiting him as often as she could while taking care of her young kids.

My immediate thought was to take chicken soup, which I had in the freezer, over to her house. But then I stopped myself, thinking I didn't want to bother her, that I wasn't close friends with her like my other neighbor was. I thought about this for a couple of days and then mustered up the courage to ring her doorbell, drop off the soup, and scatter away quickly. (Ding and dash!)

I walked over to her house and rang the doorbell. When she answered I thrust out my arm with the chicken soup. I was ready to make the dash back home, but she started to talk to me. She wanted me to stay for a few minutes. We talked about her brother's situation and she thanked me for the soup and for thinking about them. I was so glad that I did it.

You see, it's about gauging the situation, trying something out, and if it doesn't seem to be what the person needs at that time, then thinking of something else you can do. There is ALWAYS something. And sometimes, that could be giving them space. Don't worry. You'll know. Don't let your inner voice convince you that you shouldn't reach out. In these cases, it is just the opposite. When someone is ill or has a family member who is ill, hearing from people who care about them can bring a little sunshine into their day. They will be so touched that you made the effort to think of them and reach out.

WHEN YOU STILL DON'T KNOW WHAT TO SAY OR DO

When you hear that someone is seriously ill or recently received a diagnosis of cancer or other disease, you sometimes hesitate to reach out because you don't know what to say. You may even unintentionally avoid them because you are so worried about saying the wrong thing. (Yeah, I've done that a few times.) You all of a sudden feel strange about interacting with your friend or bumping into an acquaintance, because things to you are now perceived to be so different.

How can you possibly talk to them about everyday things like you used to, when their world has been turned upside down?

But this is the time to do the opposite and continue to be a friend. This is when they may need you the most. They may not want to talk about their illness or their family member's illness. Or they may. Take the lead from them when you reach out. It could be that talking about everyday "normal" stuff is what they need as a distraction or to keep things a bit "normal" for them. Who doesn't like a good yenta session once in a while?

There is no right or wrong here, so long as you are showing them that you are there for them. Or maybe they just need you to listen and be silent on the phone as they talk.

> *On my first day dropping my son off at school in Singapore after he had recently completed chemo treatment in the US, a friend found me crying outside the school and stopped to hug me.*

She apologized for never reaching out to me the months we went through his testing and treatment. She said, "I didn't know the right things to say, so I didn't say anything." That statement resonated with me to this day and made me find ways to build a program for that school so others don't feel isolated and to teach friends to reach out regardless of finding those 'perfect' words of support. (Carrie K.)

I often immediately go into "advice mode." My mom and aunt do this all the time as well. We can't help ourselves. Some people may want your advice, but most likely in a critical or traumatic situation, they already have other people and doctors giving them advice, so why would they need more from you? They need your comfort and support, not advice and stories of other people you know who have gone through similar things. So try to zip it and just be there for them.

Recently, my friend's dad was seriously ill in the hospital, in a different city than where she lived. Due to COVID-19 travel and hospital visit restrictions, she was separated from him and the rest of her family, stuck in her home, relying on updates. In the beginning I would text her daily, asking how her dad was, and call her. She's more of a texter than a phone person. During a particularly scary period in her dad's illness, she texted that things were not looking good. Instinctively, I picked up the phone to call her. Our conversation ranged from her telling me a little bit about her dad's situation to asking me to just stop talking and stay with her on the phone in silence. She said she knew that was weird, but she just needed to feel me there but didn't want to talk or have me talk. So that's what we did. I waited until she was ready to speak again before we said goodbye for that day.

Another time we spoke on the phone, I asked as usual how her dad was doing. She gave me a short update then requested we talk about anything else at all. She needed a distraction. It jarred me a bit, trying to think quickly of a "light" topic. We ultimately talked about which TV shows and books we were enjoying.

> At one point my husband was injured. It was quite serious. I received support from many people, some of whom were just acquaintances. It was a very refreshing feeling to feel the love and support. When someone I didn't expect reached out to me, it made me feel energized and optimistic. Sometimes you are not even sure if people really know you, but then they come out of the woodwork to show support, which is amazing! (Shari T.)

When someone is battling a serious illness or recovering from a surgery, it affects the entire family. The day-to-day normalcy of daily life gets thrown off-kilter. With drives to doctor appointments, or the main cook in the house or a child being sick, there just doesn't seem to be enough time in the day to do the basic things you need to do to keep a family running. The same is true when caring for an ill elderly parent, as your time and efforts are refocused on taking care of them.

I try to be specific in my offer of help versus the general "what can I do?" Sometimes people don't want to bother you, so that's why they don't take you up on your offer. But if you are already at the grocery store or picking up lunch at a restaurant, then it's easier for the person you are offering to help to accept it. Send a text like "I'm going to the grocery store. Send me your shopping list." Or, "I'm picking up lunch for myself;

I'm going to get you the sandwich and salad you like and drop it off."

> *I never hesitate. I always reach out and offer a specific task. For example: "I'm making a batch of squash soup. Can I drop a liter off?" or "I'm going grocery shopping anyway; can I get a few things for you?" And my favorite—I love to drop off a "goodie bag" of magazines, hand cream, and a treat with a card to let them know I'm thinking of them. All of these things don't take long to do and are so appreciated. (Sharon N.)*

If they have children at home or aging parents they help take care of, offer to help them with the things you know they typically do (e.g., driving a parent to a doctor appointment, or a child to a sports practice).

> *When my dad was passing (he was unconscious in intensive care for six weeks), my friends helped out by taking my kids to some of their activities and also dropping off meals. I was training for a half marathon at the time and my girlfriend would make sure I got in two runs a week and she accompanied me on some of my runs at 11 p.m. at night. (Debra B.)*

MENSCH THINGS YOU CAN DO

- Send a meal. That is one less thing they need to think about for their family and will help them out so much. Think of their favorite foods, something you know they will like.

- Buy a gift card to a local restaurant.
- Send flowers. If they have a favorite flower or color, incorporate that. Being personal is the key here rather than being generic. They will know that you are thinking specifically of them.
- Send a gift card for an online retailer such as Amazon or iTunes, so they can order what they wish, such as a book, music, etc. Or send them a selection of books that you feel will be meaningful during this time. You can also send them a selection of your favorite books that have gotten you through difficult times.
- Think of the little things that the person typically indulges in (e.g., chocolate, baths, crossword puzzles) and send them a special treat.
- If you want to check in regularly with someone who is ill, but find it hard to always remember, put it in your calendar as an ongoing reminder to call or text.
- Pay to have their house cleaned.
- Drive them to doctor appointments.
- Bring food for their family at the hospital if that is appropriate for their situation.

TO VISIT OR NOT TO VISIT?

That is the question.

The answer?

It depends.

I have two stories that illustrate different situations that required different actions.

The first one involved my mom's first cousin, Meyer. We have a very small extended family whom we are close with, and

Meyer is like a brother to my mom and aunt. I met Meyer when I was twelve years old and he moved to Toronto from Israel, so I have been close to him now for most of my life. He subsequently met his wife in Toronto and they had three amazing kids, my youngest cousins.

Last spring Meyer's second daughter, Tamar, was getting married and I drove into Toronto a few days ahead of the wedding to spend more time with my family. I arrived on a Wednesday and no sooner did I get to my brother's house than my mom called to tell us terrible news. Meyer was in the hospital and it was serious.

Like a lightning bolt the news was transmitted to my brothers as well, and we all literally dropped everything to rush to the hospital. I got there first with my sister-in-law, Vimi. Meyer was happy to see us and we sat on either side of his bed, holding his hand and talking with him. Then my mom, dad, and aunt arrived. Vimi and I left the room to let my mom and aunt go in. That's when things started getting shaky. You see, the three of them got so emotional (understandably) that monitors started beeping as Meyer's emotions overcame him. They called the nurses and we all stood out of the room in the hallway.

By that time my brothers had arrived at the hospital as well. We all realized that while we wanted to be there for Meyer and his family, it wasn't best for our cousin. He had his wife, children, and their significant others with him, and as much as we felt the need to be there ourselves, it was doing more harm than good. So we sat downstairs in the hospital café and agreed we would not come back to the hospital again until his immediate family said it was a good idea.

But of course, I didn't leave it there. A couple days later, as the wedding was approaching quickly, I reached out by text to Meyer's daughter, who wasn't the one getting married. I offered to stay with him at the hospital so they could prepare for the wedding and all the upcoming festivities. I left it at that. I guess I was pushy, but tried not to be *too* pushy.

I was surprised to receive a call from my cousin's wife later that day. She was very direct. "We would like you to stay with Meyer on Friday while we are at the Shabbat dinner for the wedding guests," she said. "And then at the wedding itself on Sunday, please be his 'helper' throughout the wedding." I immediately agreed.

I felt needed and they took me up on my offer. It definitely was more about me—as I needed to feel useful, helpful. I just hope that I helped them a little bit too.

My second story is quite different. On a different visit to Toronto, I told my mom that Sunday would be "all hers" for me to spend with her and do whatever she wanted to do. She didn't need to think long about it, and asked me to go with her to visit her dying friend and then go to visit my *Tante* Bala at the nursing home. *Tante* Bala was my bubbie's youngest and only surviving sister.

tante
/tan-teh/
n. aunt

Mom said we would only stay a few minutes at each visit.

No lunch? No going downtown to walk and shop? Nope, not with my mom. She wanted me to help her comfort others. That's my mom.

On that Sunday, I got into my mom's car and she pointed to two plants in the back seat that she had bought for me to give to her friend and Tante Bala. Yup, she always has it all covered. We drove first to her friend's house. I braced myself as we approached the front door. I knew that her friend was in palliative care at home and the situation was very bad. His wife, my mom's good friend, opened the door and gave me a huge hug.

She guided us into the family room, where her husband lay in a hospital bed, sleeping. I bent over his bed to say hello while he was resting.

Then we went into the kitchen and she wanted to make us tea and serve us some sweets. I was hesitant to stay, as I thought we would be bothering her during such an intimate, stressful time. An hour later, we told her we needed to leave to go to our next visit.

You see, my mom's friend needed us around her. She needed to talk, and so we took her cues and stayed for a while longer to be with her.

Lessons Learned from These Experiences

- You can offer to visit someone in the hospital but only if they are OK with it.
- When visiting, limit the length of your visit as they need their rest.
- Don't bring young children to visit someone who is recovering from a surgery unless that person has expressly asked you to. They need time to rest and recuperate.

Neighbors dropped off dinner for us the day we got back from the hospital after my husband's back surgery. Many messages and offers to help in these types of situations made me feel like people cared and wanted to help out. But I will add, many will reach out and say, "Let me know if you need any help," but we rarely will take people up on it since we do not want to impose. So I think the best cases are when people just do something to show they care. Send a get-well package, send food, etc. (Natalia Y.)

Cousins of mine whom I don't regularly speak to on the phone made the effort to call and leave me messages after hearing that I had had surgery and suffered complications. I felt loved and cared for. (Laurie L.)

Always remember that showing your support will mean so much to the recipient, especially when it's coming from someone unexpected.

A woman from my synagogue was in a coma for weeks and then having a slow recovery. I didn't find out until she was already at home. I brought her soup and conversation several times while she was recovering. I'm her personal soup chef! (Alia C.)

Grand gestures aren't necessary. Simply sending a message or a handwritten card with words of encouragement to show you're thinking of them can add a bit of brightness to someone's day. Reach out to show your support! You won't regret it. And it's the mensch thing to do.

CHAPTER NINE

Get Over Yourself and Off Your *Tuches*

Do you ever procrastinate? I totally do. A lot. It's usually things that I don't like to do, or that make me uncomfortable. Why would I do it right away if I could just wait another day? Tomorrow, tomorrow.

I can give you an entire list of things that I procrastinate about, but that would take up this whole book. Making a dentist appointment, doing work on a tough project, and the list goes on and on. So I'll try to focus on one area that really causes me stress when I procrastinate. And that's when I mean to send a donation to someone who lost a loved one. I really want to, but for some reason, I keep putting it off. Unfortunately, I've done this a lot. I even put it in my calendar. Then that day I move it to the next day, or the next week.

Here's a big one that caused me a lot of stress a couple of years ago. It's a situation that still sits with me today. Every Passover we do the first-night Seder with my husband's side of the family. This is the one time a year that we see his aunt's sister and her family. And every year, I have seen and really noticed her sons grow from little boys into strapping, handsome, and kind young men. I look forward to seeing and catching up with their family as we are seated across from them at the table.

The brother-in-law passed away a couple of years ago, shortly after one of our Passover Seders. We had just spent the holiday with them, and it was so nice to have our annual catch-up. Since they live in Toronto, and we are in New Jersey, we did not go to the funeral or shiva. I planned to send a memorial donation and card to his widow.

Days went by, then months, and I don't know why, but I didn't get around to doing it. Every once in a while the thought would pop into my head, but I had so many other things on my daily to-do lists that I just didn't get to it.

Nearly a year after he passed, the next Passover approached and I started to get anxious. I was going to see his widow and sons at the upcoming Seder and still had not sent my condolences. I felt terrible, thinking it was too late and how would I face them.

Would I say, "Sorry to hear about your husband/dad" *almost a year later*? Or would I just have casual conversations and ignore that it had happened at all? I didn't like either of these scenarios. They made me feel even worse.

I finally mustered up my courage and decided it wasn't too late to do something to offer my condolences. It was certainly better than not doing anything at all. I looked up his obituary online and saw where the family had requested memorial donations to be sent and I sent one from my family.

Did his wife or kids mention this when I saw them at the Seder? No, they didn't. But they didn't need to. And I didn't need an acknowledgment. I needed to know for myself that

I had finally followed through with what I had originally intended to do, which was to express my sympathy to them.

There are so many reasons why we don't reach out immediately to support someone when we fully have good intentions to do so.

A million reasons.

And then, there are just no reasons. We really have no idea why we haven't done it yet. And it festers and festers. Once in a while it'll pop up in our minds. Maybe someone will mention that friend, and it will remind us that we still haven't reached out.

And it drives us meshugenah.

Many of us have been in this situation. We hear of a friend or acquaintance who is ill or has lost a loved one and we want to reach out to them, but then days go by and we forget or life just gets in the way. Then more time goes by and we feel like too much time has passed and it's just plain awkward.

Or maybe we find out about someone who was very ill or lost a family member, and it was months ago. But we only heard about it recently. We may think that too much time has passed, but again, it's never too late to show our support and offer words of comfort.

Here's another situation where, quite honestly, I felt like a total schmuck.

When we were living in Singapore, I heard through friends that a former classmate of my son's was battling cancer. She was around ten years old at that time. I really liked her parents. We were friends, not best friends, but definitely friends. Prior to moving, we weren't in touch regularly, but always loved seeing one another when we occasionally did.

When I heard the news about their daughter, I thought about them and all that they must be going through. I meant to reach out to them but never did. Then I just felt so awkward that too much time had passed that I didn't do anything.

Two years later we moved back from Singapore to New Jersey and I went out for coffee with my friend. We hadn't been in touch at all while we were away. It was so good to see her and our conversation flowed smoothly—just like it always had before.

After about half an hour I took a deep breath and told her how bad I felt that I had never reached out to support and acknowledge her when her daughter was fighting cancer. She sat silently and listened to me.

There was no "it's OK, don't worry."

Because really, that wasn't warranted at all. But I was so appreciative that she listened to me. I had worried about it for so long and still to this day regret that I didn't reach out. I learned from this experience to now do things differently in similar situations (or try to).

It's never too late to show your support. Of course it's better to not procrastinate, but if you do, you should still try to reach out. Get off your tuches, take a deep breath, and go for it.

MENSCH THINGS YOU CAN DO

- Write a personalized note through a Facebook message, text, or email, or mail a card. Make sure it's personal and not something posted to the public. This will have deeper meaning. Say "I know you've gone through a hard time and I just want to let you know I've been thinking of you."
- Send flowers, a gift basket, or a treat with a note expressing "hope this brightens your day a little." This unexpected gesture will surely bring warmth that they are supported and loved.
- Send a donation in memory of the person who passed away. Or if they are ill, a donation to an

organization that raises funds for the illness they have.

Sometimes it is awkward because you aren't close and you don't know what to say or do, but it is always better to offer and let them turn you down than to not offer at all. Again, respect their privacy but let them know you are there for them. If I hesitate and I am still thinking about it a day or two later, I reach out because there is no harm. (Robyn F.)

I don't hesitate. I always reach out if I know about it, and if I find out late, I call and tell them I just found out. Life is too short to be too busy to reach out to people who matter to you. (Donna K.)

YOU FEEL SO AWKWARD

As we've talked about earlier, death and serious illness are tough. They suck. And it's awkward when we need to face them to comfort someone else.

That's just life.

Our choice is to shy away from it or embrace it and reach out.

I get really uncomfortable in these situations. What's funny is that my friends don't think I do. They think I'm just very outgoing and good in most situations. I guess I put on a good game face, because believe me, I get anxiety and fear too. I think what they see is the result after I try my very best to push myself out of my comfort zone. This is not easy. But I try. Just a little bit at a time. You can too.

Here's one situation I found myself in.

The principal of my kids' elementary school lost his sister and was sitting shiva. I was by no means good friends with him, but whenever we would see each other, at someone's gathering, or on visiting day at our kids' camp, we always chatted. When I heard about him sitting shiva, I was in a quandary about whether or not I should pay a shiva visit. I finally decided that I would go. I parked my car in front of his house and felt, literally, anxious. I wasn't sure if I would know anyone there, and if I did know people, would they think it was weird that I was there?

I mustered up my courage and went into the house.

At first, my fears and anxieties came true. I didn't know where to stand, where to go, where to sit. And I saw a friend of mine who looked at me in surprise and literally said to me, "What are you doing here? I didn't expect to see you here."

I felt I needed to justify why I showed up, rambling on about how we occasionally bumped into each other, and so on. Then I saw the mourner sitting in the living room, waited for the person he was speaking with to move on, and approached him to express my condolences. We had a really nice conversation. We talked about his sister. He asked how my kids were doing.

He was appreciative that I came. And then I made a quick exit. Once outside I let out a huge sigh, glad it was over, glad I did it, and drove home.

WHO IN THE WORLD IS *THAT* PERSON?

Like there wasn't enough to worry about, here's another one. Sorry. (The Canadian in me always feels the need to apologize. Sorry again.)

What in the world do you do when someone you know has passed away and you want to pay your respects, but you only knew them at work, for instance, and don't know their family at all? You're kind of stuck—grieving the death of your friend or coworker, but at a loss over how to express this to their family to honor them and pay your respects.

Talk about awkward. Going to a visitation. By yourself. Lining up to greet the mourners, then introducing yourself to them. Walking away and seeing people congregating, not knowing if you should just sort of stand there by yourself or make a quick getaway.

If you've ever attended a funeral by yourself, you know it can be extra uncomfortable. No one is saving a seat for you. You don't know where to sit, what to do with yourself.

Oy! Not fun at all.

I've been in this situation. First thing I do is find a seat close to the back of the chapel or visitation room. Then I sit quietly and try to focus on my breath to calm my nerves down. I read the memorial booklet that was distributed. I try to just sit and breathe until the service starts.

Once the service begins, it's much easier as the focus is on the service at the front of the room and you're not as self-conscious that people may be looking at you, wondering who the heck you are. By the way, I can almost guarantee that they aren't looking at you as intently as you think. They are most likely just as uncomfortable as you are—fidgeting, looking around, trying to find distractions. Or maybe they *are* looking at you, wondering who you are. But what can you do? Get over yourself. You can handle it.

When people are mourning, hearing stories about the person they've lost, from people in their lives whom they don't know, can bring a smile, a warmth to them about how their loved one had touched someone else's life. It can be extremely comforting. They may not know you personally, but receiving a card or a message with a story is an amazing feeling.

I typically write to close friends and family who lose someone. I have also tried to keep the appropriate "space" for the person, not wanting to intrude. I have, on occasion, procrastinated on the time to write or reach out and this has usually been that while I may deeply miss the person who has passed, my relationship with the mourner isn't as close and therefore I find it harder to write something meaningful to them. (George K.)

I was touched by some letters and cards I received when my brother passed away. I was especially touched by the stories people shared about my brother. (Abby B.)

It isn't for everyone to do this. And that's OK. You don't have to overcome super anxiety and conquer all your fears by going in person.

But you aren't off the hook just yet! This is when you can make other meaningful gestures to express your condolences and honor your friend. Send a donation in memory of them. It doesn't have to be a lot of money. In this case, "it's the thought that counts" has even more gravitas because "it's the action that counts."

BUT YOU STAY UPDATED FROM OTHER PEOPLE

There are times when you know that the person who is experiencing the difficulty is overwhelmed, and the right thing for you to do is to not bother them at all. So you stay updated on their situation from other people. Having one point person communicate to their "village" is perfect for the person enduring a tough time who really needs space.

But this doesn't mean you can't do anything. You don't need to reach out directly by phone or text. Simply mail them a card. Again, you aren't off the hook to do nothing. There is always *something* appropriate in every situation that can bring comfort to people.

OY GEVALT! WHAT IF THEY ASK YOU FOR THINGS YOU CAN'T OR DON'T WANT TO DO?

This is a real fear. What if you offer "what can I do to help?" and your friend asks you to drive their kids every Monday and Wednesday to soccer practice. But you don't think you can manage it since you work full-time and have to drive your own kids to their activities those days?

Awkward.

Now how do you get out of this pickle you got yourself in without being a total schmuck?

You already have so much on your plate that you yourself are drowning; you're just too busy. Or you are financially strapped. You worry that if you offer to help someone, they may ask you for something you aren't able to do, find uncomfortable, or just plainly don't want to do.

In these situations, my best advice is to offer something specific when you reach out. Don't keep it open-ended. No vague "let me know what I can do." Instead, be very specific about how you want to help them so that you are comfortable with it as well. Your offer is something you know can help them, but also something that you can do.

SHE DID BUBKES FOR YOU

Expectations. We all have them of the people we are close to. These expectations are often the most tested when we are going through a rough time. We expect that those close to us will step up and reach out. But this isn't always the case, and we get hurt.

When a friend is going through a difficult time, sometimes we can't help ourselves, but we immediately think, *What have they done for me?* It just flashes into our minds. We then evaluate our relationship with that person. Perhaps we make a mental chart of the things they've done for us, or haven't done. How we might have been disappointed with them in a reverse similar situation.

> *One very good friend did very little to help me when I was sick, which surprised me. She rarely reached out. I have moved past this and just think that she must have been going through something as well. What also surprised me were the people that I didn't know very well who ended up going above and beyond for me, because they understood what I was going through. (Cathleen M.)*

I've been so fortunate in my life that I feel very supported by my village of friends and family. However, there have been times when I've felt let down by a friend. And then the tables turn, and my friend needs support. I've reached out to my mom during these times and her question to me has been "What would you have done to help your friend had you not felt hurt by her previously? Do what you would normally do. Kindness will breed kindness."

I do my best to follow this great advice.

There are surely going to be times when you feel disappointed and hurt—and then you are called upon to be there for that same person. Yes, you may be hurt—we are all human—but remember that you will feel even better when you follow your first instinct and reach out to support them.

Be ready to forgive and forget. Maybe it will help if you say to yourself, "I'll be the bigger person."

Do what YOU think is the right thing to do. And then move on and be that awesome, kind, caring person you are.

THERE ARE SO MANY OPPORTUNITIES TO GET INSULTED

Have you ever had any of these thoughts or feelings?

"I was the last to know . . ."

"Why didn't you tell me sooner?"

"Why did they find out before me?"

"I was the last person to hear that he is sick."

"She answered her text, but not mine."

It feels pretty crappy when you are left out of the loop. Especially if you thought you were close to someone and they didn't choose you to reach out to, to confide in, to update on this serious event in their lives.

It's important to try to put your empathy hat on in these situations and remember that it's about them, not you. Try your best to give them the benefit of the doubt. They may be so overwhelmed with their stressful, difficult situation that they cannot get themselves together enough to reach out to everyone in their circle. This isn't the time to get insulted or be hurt. Turn it around and be supportive of your friend or family member.

Move on. Be kind.

WE'VE BEEN THROUGH THIS, NOW WE KNOW

I've made so many missteps along the way. Didn't reach out to someone when I heard they lost a parent, or when they experienced a serious illness. I've shared some of these stories with you earlier. One thing I've found by talking to people who have experienced loss or serious illness is that they also didn't always reach out to others before. But after dealing with it themselves, they changed their approach.

Some of us thankfully haven't dealt with losing a close family member or battling a serious illness, so we don't know what to do when these things happen to people we know. We hesitate, procrastinate, make all the mistakes we've talked about before. But many people, once they have experienced these situations, are more inclined to reach out when they hear of others going through them. Because they now "get it." When you have gone through it yourself, you gain a whole new perspective.

> *I think many people don't know what to say. When my mother passed away, close friends reached out, while many other people in my life didn't do that. It made me realize that I need to contact anyone who has lost a loved one. It is comforting to feel connected during that kind of grief. (Jacquie M.)*

> *Many people don't know how to respond or what to do or what to say. While I was disappointed, I knew not to take it personally. Until you've experienced a profound loss, you truly don't understand and I couldn't expect others to understand. Prior to losing my father, I may have hesitated. After losing my father and knowing what it was like, I no longer hesitate or procrastinate. I just do. (Robyn F.)*

TRY NOT TO JUDGE OTHERS

Etiquette. What is appropriate in all these situations? Guess what? There's no clear answer to this question. It all depends on the situation. There are always going to be people who criticize and judge others' actions. It's like they get off on it. It's their *shtick*.

shtick
/sh-tick/
n. something you are known for doing

And there are always lots of yentas chatting after a funeral. It gives them something to talk about with their friends afterward. Perhaps they talk about everyone and everything else to shift the conversation away from their own discomfort and sorrow about the person who passed away. You may have overheard others saying things such as:

"Did you see what her nephew wore to the funeral? He must be meshugenah to think that was OK to wear. Such a shame he never got married."

"OMG, did you see who showed up at the funeral? Her ex-husband with his new *tchotchkala*. I heard she was his *yoga* teacher. Private lessons, I'm sure."

tchotchkala
/cht-utch-ka-la/
n. a tart, a floozy

"The daughter-in-law didn't even show up for the funeral. So what that they don't talk. What a *shande!*"

shande

/shan-DEH/

n. a disgrace

"Did you see how he pushed himself to the front of the line at the buffet and how much lox he took? What a schnorrer!"

My brothers and I have our own shtick that after one of us goes to a funeral, we talk about the shoes that people wore to the cemetery. My brother Avrum calls them "cemetery shoes" and doesn't understand why some women choose to wear heels when they know they will be walking on cemetery grass, wobbling along as their heels dig into the ground. It's even worse if it is raining or snowing, or the ground is just simply wet.

I have definitely been judgmental myself about etiquette. I had always thought to never bring a baby to a funeral, shiva, or visitation. It's just not appropriate.

"She brought the baby to the shiva? Couldn't stop crying. *Oy, abrocht!*"

When my daughter Sydnee was only a few months old, my mom's friend's father passed away. My mom (as usual) wanted me to accompany her on a shiva visit *and* wanted me to bring the baby with us. I was aghast, telling my mom that it wasn't appropriate to bring a baby to a shiva. My mom vehemently disagreed, and as typically happens, I succumbed to my mom's wishes and brought the baby along.

We walked up to the front door, me whispering to baby Sydnee in her car seat bucket to be as quiet as a mouse (not that a baby would oblige!) and dangling the bucket slightly behind me so as not to be conspicuous.

What happened next totally surprised me. The elderly widow welcomed us with a huge smile and open arms. "Bring me the baby," she said to me. My baby daughter had the perfect response, smiling and cooing right back at her. For the short time we visited that afternoon, the baby brought the grieving widow a few moments of comfort and joy that only a baby can.

I've thought a lot about this encounter and if it is really appropriate to bring young children to pay a condolence visit. This is where I've netted out. In short, yes, it is quite OK to do so. Children can often bring a sense of levity and joy to a shiva or visitation. Seeing a baby smile and talking with a child can momentarily ease the family's pain.

However, if you do decide to bring a young child or baby to a shiva or visitation, please be aware that if your child becomes fussy, do not overstay your welcome. Use your sekhel (common sense) and you can't go wrong.

CHAPTER TEN

They Are Being So Difficult

Every now and then, we encounter a situation when a friend or family member is going through a very rough time and it is difficult to lend them a hand. And it's really frustrating. It is often not that they don't *want* the help, it is that they are so overwhelmed with the situation and emotions they are dealing with that they can't wrap their head around getting help. In their mind, thinking about where they need help is almost harder than accepting the help.

When my friend Ariel's father passed away suddenly, I immediately made arrangements to fly to Ottawa to attend the funeral. I was so stressed out because I could only stay for one night and one day due to obligations back at home. I wanted to be there for her longer but simply couldn't. Nonetheless, I was determined to pack in as much "help and support" as I could in those twenty-four hours.

The morning of the funeral, I went to her parents' house with another close friend of hers, Katharine. We made a pact that if we sensed we shouldn't be there, we would leave. But on the other hand, we wanted to be there in case they did want us. Both of us needed to leave after the funeral, yet we wanted to spend as much time as we possibly could and do anything for Ariel and her family.

We arrived at the house and hugged Ariel deeply, and then I jumped into "what can I do to help?" mode. They were still in a state of shock and trauma over the sudden loss of their husband and father and couldn't articulate anything for me to do.

After a while her mom said, "Elisa, come help me put the tablecloth on the table. I know you really want and need to do something."

A light went off in my head and I realized, *Sh*t. I'm making this about me!* As I laid out the tablecloth, I started to think, *It's so not about me right now, but about them. What in heaven's name am I doing? What should I do now?*

Ariel, bless her heart, gave us an errand to do for her at the nearby mall. Katharine and I talked in the car and decided that we really needed to give them space and leave after we dropped off what Ariel asked us to get. When we got back to the house after doing the errand, the family was about to go for a walk to get some fresh air before the funeral.

That was our cue to leave—and we took it.

IT'S NOT ABOUT YOU, IT'S ABOUT THEM

If you encounter a similar situation, when you really want to do something and offer your help and the person doesn't take you up on it, remember my golden rule for mensches: IT'S NOT ABOUT YOU, IT'S ABOUT THEM.

Take their cues and try your best to respect their wishes. And don't get insulted. You will likely feel at a loss and go a little meshugenah yourself as you feel helpless that you can't do more to support them. It doesn't mean you aren't a good friend or a good family member. It's just that they can't take it right then. As time goes by, reach out again. They may be more open to receiving help later. Or they may not. You'll see.

Their job in these times is to take care of their family and themselves, not to make you feel better!

It's your job to take the pressure off and do your best to make it about them and their needs, and not about you and making yourself feel better. So many of us feel we need to do something. That's what I'm like, and it's so hard for me when I want to offer support and the person doesn't want it. It just makes me feel useless.

WHY WON'T THEY ACCEPT YOUR HELP?

It is important to try to understand why you think people won't accept help. Are they extremely private? Do they get overwhelmed easily? Are they too upset to even think straight in that moment? Do they feel like the support would just complicate things? Do they worry too much about inconveniencing others?

Take the time to sit back and think about them and their situation. Put your energies into understanding them better. Have empathy for them instead of focusing on what YOU can do.

> *I understand when people don't want help . . . everyone processes illnesses/death differently. I find it is important to listen and pay attention to their body language and to check in with them frequently to know that help is always available should they want it. (Debra B.)*

There is a plethora of reasons why someone may rebuff you or not take you up on your offer of help and support at a particular time. They could be inundated with too many calls and texts from well-meaning friends and family and literally cannot keep up with answering everyone. This doesn't mean that they don't appreciate you reaching out. Perhaps you offer to bring over dinner and they say no thank you. Maybe their fridge and freezer are already packed and bursting. This is a blessing, as they have more than enough food to help them out and it's one less thing for them to worry about. But it does get to a point when there's too much, it becomes stressful for the person to find places to store your delicious meals, and they worry the food will go bad.

> *Everyone started bringing food and then a friend offered and I was like, "Please, no more food!" Maybe they could have offered to take one of the kids for a while or take clothes to the cleaners. There are many things people need other than food when going through a crisis. (Anne H.)*

Some people, by their nature, worry about a lot of things, especially inconveniencing others.

> *I usually never want anyone to go to any trouble. Plus I am never good at anticipating my needs. (Brett S.)*

Keeping busy is another coping strategy for some people. They want to do things themselves. It's their way of coping.

> *One of my colleagues offered to help me with some of my workload, which was very appreciated, but I actually had better days when I was busy and*

kept my mind working. I needed hugs. I needed
space. I did not need less to do. (Jessica C.)

Or they are doing everything they can to stay strong and feel accepting help is a weakness because it shows them this is very real and they aren't ready to accept it yet? With time, they may realize that they do need help. But in the beginning they are just fighting for their own survival.

> *I like being independent. While in mourning, peo-*
> *ple were constantly trying to help. While this*
> *sounds like a good thing to most people, I couldn't*
> *stand having to fight my way to get my own cup of*
> *coffee or empty the dishwasher. They could have*
> *simply let me be, and stood next to me, keeping*
> *up with conversation, etc. (Amanda W.)*

Everyone reacts differently when faced with stressful situations. Some people need others around them all the time, while others may need time to be alone. It's so individual.

> *Sometimes you just feel you want to be alone, so*
> *you kindly pass on the help. Although, nice ges-*
> *tures are always well received! (Shari T.)*

HOW TO BE THOUGHTFUL AND SUPPORTIVE WITHOUT BEING A NOODGE

When you are faced with this kind of situation, and you really want to support the person going through a difficult time, try your best not to pressure them too much and be a *noodge*. This will only add to their stress. *Losen gein* (leave them be).

noodge
/noodge/
n. a pest
v. to pester, to nag

Don't take it personally. It's not about you, it's about them. Don't get offended if your offer to visit with them or take over a meal is turned down.

It's OK to ask more than once and offer a few different things. But it is important not to be too pushy. Read the situation. If your efforts are turned down, then you can find other ways to show your support that aren't intrusive. If you push too much, you risk causing your friend or family member increased stress, and it will affect your relationship. Respect their wishes.

NON-NOODGE, MENSCH THINGS YOU CAN DO

When your offers of help are not accepted, and you really want to do something without being too much of a noodge, here are a few unobtrusive ways you can show them you care:

- Text or email a personalized note saying, "I know you're going through a hard time and I just want to let you know I'm thinking of you and I'm here for you. No need to reply."
- Write a note in a beautiful or cute greeting card and mail it to their home. Or email them a greeting card.
- Send flowers or a gift basket with a brief note like "Hope this brightens your day a little."
- Mail or email them a gift card to a local restaurant so they can order in dinner when they need it.

- Send them a little *nosh*, cookies, or another treat they will enjoy.

Sometimes you don't realize the power of a card or message from people—or the value of a simple memory of your loved one—until the card arrives. (Cindy R.)

ACCEPTING HELP IS AS IMPORTANT AS GIVING IT

If you find yourself saying "I don't need any help" more often than saying "yes" when someone offers help, then you may be the type of person who finds it easy to support others but difficult when others want to reciprocate.

My mom and I constantly have friction when I want to do something to help her or even just be kind and do something nice for her and she doesn't want to take me up on it. She does that same thing with my brothers. It frustrates us to no end! She's a "giver" and it's really hard for her to be the "taker" or recipient of others' help.

My parents are both extremely generous people. When my brothers and I became adults who actually earned a living (finally!), we wanted to treat our parents to gifts, dinners out, etc. But oh, was it difficult to do with our mom. She made it *very* difficult. This is how a typical conversation with her would go:

ME: Mom, when you and Dad come to New Jersey, we want to take you out for dinner to celebrate your birthdays.
MOM: Nice idea.

I gave her the heads-up, no? Didn't I say WE wanted to take THEM out for dinner?

This is what happened. I made a reservation for the six of us (including the grandchildren, of course) at a special restaurant that I had been to once before. It's called Ninety Acres and is situated on a beautiful estate, serving up local fare with a casual, chic atmosphere. And it's on the expensive side, which means special occasions only—which this was, as we were taking my parents out to celebrate their sixty-fifth birthdays.

We walked into the restaurant and my parents started commenting on how nice it looked, already seemingly impressed with my choice.

The server brought the menus to our table. I took my mom's menu out of her hands and put it facedown on the table before she could look at the prices.

> ME: Mom, don't forget, this is *our* treat. We are paying for dinner.
> MOM: No, no, that is not necessary.
> ME: Please let me do this.
> MOM: But why? You have so many expenses, the kids' school, camp . . .
> ME: You and Dad paid for my and my brothers' braces, summer camp, skiing lessons, and so much more. You guys never took a vacation except for an annual road trip. PLEASE, don't fight me.
> MOM: OK, Elisa. FINE.

Before I gave the menu back to my mom, our conversation went like this:

> ME: OK, Mom, this can go one of two ways. I don't want you to look at the prices and order the cheapest thing on the menu. If you don't think you can do that, then I will read the menu to

you, and you can choose what you'd like to order
from my description.
MOM: I can HANDLE looking at the menu. Pass me
the menu, please.

We had an incredible dinner.

My parents talked about that dinner and how nice it was
for so long after. Since then, my mom and I have had many conversations when she wasn't feeling well, or my dad wasn't, and
I wanted to send them something (I wasn't living in Toronto
near them), and she would tell me no, they didn't want me to.
I explained to her that she gives so much to others and to me,
and it feels good, right? Please give me the opportunity to feel
good too. And by the way, Mom, the same thing goes for my
brothers and sisters-in-law when they want to do something
nice for you and Dad too. Please let us.

You see, I finally decided to meet this head-on and confront her about how this makes me and my brothers feel. I gave
her examples of when she did something for one of us and
asked her how it made her feel. She told me it made her feel
good, happy, and useful. I then told her that we also want to
feel this way sometimes. And I asked her to please give us the
gift of accepting our help occasionally as well.

It is easy to mistake accepting help for weakness. Some
people are fiercely independent and feel that if they accept any
help they are being weak, letting themselves down because
they think to themselves, *I can handle this. I don't need anyone.* Accepting help makes them feel vulnerable.

When you are in the position of people wanting to support
and help you, my suggestion is to embrace your vulnerability
and see it as a strength to do so. You are brave to show others
that you are human. It will make them feel even better about
themselves when they accept help from you the next time.

When you accept help from another, you are giving that person an opportunity to give. It is truly a gift you are giving to that person. You are helping them feel purposeful and appreciated for the things they do for you. You also let them in and allow them to become more connected to you. Your relationships will only strengthen as you gain the ability and willingness to receive as well as to give.

Here are a few things you can say to make it easier to accept help from people when your first reaction is to reject it:

- "Right now I am overwhelmed, but I really appreciate you reaching out. Perhaps in a couple of weeks I'll be readier to accept your help. I know I'll need it."
- "Thank you for your offer to bring over dinner. Right now we are overloaded with food and it's just too much. It would be wonderful if you don't mind checking back with me in a few weeks and I would really appreciate a dinner then."
- "We don't really eat fish. However, if you would like to make chicken, that would be wonderful."
- "At this moment, we really need privacy. Please don't take this the wrong way. I will be open to meeting for a coffee or a visit in a few weeks. Thank you so much for understanding."

CONCLUSION

Unleash Your Inner Mensch

I know you are already a mensch because you picked up this book and got to the end!

Being a mensch is a mindset rather than a "one and done" in a specific situation. Embrace the good intentions and love inside you to unleash even more of your kindness to bestow upon others.

My hope is that you now have even more ideas that you can incorporate into your daily life and are better prepared in how to react or take action in new uncomfortable situations where you can make a positive impact on someone else.

You won't get it "perfect" all the time. No one does. Be good to yourself, kind to yourself. If you find you made a misstep, there's always a way to correct it. People are by nature understanding and kind and will give you back the love you send them.

Go get 'em!

ACKNOWLEDGMENTS

First and foremost my gratitude goes to my friend Tamara Stieber, who taught and guided me in how to transform my thoughts into the written word. I will be forever grateful to her for the honest, thoughtful, and direct conversations we had and for being the catalyst in pointing out to me to "be me" when writing this book, embracing my inner balaboosta and authentic voice to share with others.

It was a pleasure to work with my editor, Patrick Price.

The team at Girl Friday Productions was fabulous to work with. Professional, insightful, and just darn good at what they do in guiding authors like me to publish their books.

Incredibly thankful for Razi Saju and David Riabov at Scratch Marketing and Stewart Caron at Atwater Media Inc. for sticking with me throughout this journey of creating caringorganizer.com. Changing careers and becoming a first-time social entrepreneur is not for the faint of heart, and these three guys always kept me up when I was down. I will always be grateful for their guidance and strategic minds, and most importantly for being mensches and kind to me when things didn't always go as planned.

Many thanks to everyone who shared their experiences with me—how they support others and have been supported—and most importantly for being candid and open in sharing how they felt in these situations.

I am so lucky to have a wonderful village of friends and family, who have lifted me up and supported me unconditionally throughout my ups and downs on this crazy journey. Grateful for these women, many of whom I've been friends with for over thirty years. Ariel Dalfen, Jacquie Morin, Beata Mehta, Terrie-Lynne Devonish, Nisa Krongold Diamond, Wendy James, Donna Cantor, Andrea Victor, Karen Rosen, Vimi Udaskin, Estée Garfin, Amanda Wener, Lauren Blankstein, Lauren Weisler, Veronica Syrtash, Dafna Carr, Sandy Kyriakatos, Sandra Olper, Sheera Siegel, Robin Einbinder Milich, Rona Epstein, Jill Petroro, Karen Landsman, Gerri Russo. My neighbors and friends Liz Szporn, Tara Bernie, Tracey Saia, Jill Betzel, and Anne Heap—who have shown me the true meaning of "it takes a village"—through good times and bad, always there to support one another.

Thankful for my brothers, Avrum Udaskin and Jamie Udaskin, and my cousins Jeremy "Yosi" Rezmovitz, David Rezmovitz, and Benji Rezmovitz, all true mensches, who continue to inspire me with their constant kindness to people, even strangers, like we were taught growing up.

I am so fortunate to have the most supportive, generous, and strong mothers-in-law, always cheering me on—Elayne Isenberg and Annette Auerbach. And in loving memory of my dear father-in-law, the original gentle giant, Jack Day.

Eternally grateful and filled with so much love for my parents, Linda and Stan Udaskin, and my aunt and uncle, Nina and Jack Rezmovitz, who raised me, guided me, and showed me from the beginning what it means to be a mensch.

Saving the best for last—the people who put up with me every day in close quarters. Thank you to my husband, Adam, and kids, Sydnee and Kobi, for hanging in there with me as I changed careers, which had a big impact on them as well as me. Adjusting from Mom always traveling and being at work to Mom being home all the time was not always easy. I love you all very much.

GLOSSARY OF YIDDISH WORDS AND EXPRESSIONS

balaboosta or balabusta—a good homemaker, a woman who's in charge of her home

bubbie—a grandmother, also spelled bubbe, boobie

bubkes—nothing; trivial, worthless, useless; a ridiculously small amount

chutzpah—In English, *chutzpah* often connotes courage or confidence, but among Yiddish speakers, it is not a compliment. Though the Yiddish word originally had an entirely negative connotation, it is now used as a slang word in everyday conversation, both positively and negatively.

ess—to eat

Gei kachen offen yam—literally, "go take a sh*t in the ocean," but is synonymous with "go take a hike" or "get outta here."

golem—a stupid and clumsy person, a blockhead

gutte neshama—a good soul

hocking a chinik—to nag

keppy—head

kinde—children

koyach—inner strength, energy, wherewithal

kreplach—dumpling

kvell—to burst with pride over the actions and accomplishments of someone else. To beam with pride and pleasure.

Jewish parents are prone to kvell over their children's achievements.

kvetch—to complain or whine. Someone who complains or whines. Verb or noun.

Lo mir gain vaiter—Now let's get on with it.

lokshen—noodles

Losen gein—Leave it alone.

Mazel tov—Congratulations!

mein kinde—my kids

mensch—an honorable, decent person; an authentic person; a person who helps you when you need help. Can be a man, woman, or child.

meshugenah—crazy, ridiculous, insane

mishegas—insanity or craziness

naches—the feeling of pride and/or gratification in the achievements of another; one's own doing good by helping someone or some organization. To *"shep naches"* means to derive pleasure.

noodge—to pester, nag, whine; as a noun, a pest or whiner; to bother, to push; a person who bothers you

nosh—to nibble; a light snack. Verb and noun.

nu—interjection that calls for a reply. It can mean "So?," "Huh?," "Well?," "What's up?," or "Hello?"

nudnik—a pest, a persistent and annoying person

ongeblozen—sulky, pouty; a sourpuss. Adjective and noun.

Oy abrocht!—interjection meaning "Oh my goodness!," "What a catastrophe!," or "What a bad thing!"

Oy vey—exclamation of dismay, grief, or exasperation. The phrase *"oy vey iz mir"* means "oh, woe is me." *"Oy gevalt!"* is like oy vey, but expresses fear, shock, or amazement.

pish—to pee, urinate

plotz—or *plats*. Literally, to explode, to collapse. To go crazy because you love something so much.

putz—a jerk or a self-made fool, but literally means penis

rachmones—compassion

schmaltzy—excessively sentimental, gushing, flattering, over the top, corny

schmuck—an obnoxious, contemptible, or detestable person; an idiot; a dickhead

schnorrer—a moocher, someone who wants to always get things for free; a parasite, someone who takes advantage of others

sekhel—common sense, good judgment

shalom ba-bayet—peace in the home

shande—a disgrace

shayna maidele—a pretty girl

shiva—the seven-day mourning ritual in Judaism

shlep—to drag, traditionally something you don't really need; to carry unwillingly. When people "shlep around," they are dragging themselves, perhaps slouching.

shmatta—a rag, old clothing

shtetl—small village

shtick—something you're known for doing

shvitz—to sweat

tante—aunt

tchotchkala—a tart, a floozy

tsuris—or *tsores*. Troubles, worries, problems.

tuches—rear end, behind

verklempt—feeling overwhelmed with a myriad of emotions. Choked up with emotion.

yenta—female busybody or gossip

yiddishkeit—Jewish way of life

yo'ach—broth

zaftig—a chubby woman

zaida—or zayde, a grandfather

ABOUT THE AUTHOR

© *Matt Epstein*

Elisa Udaskin is a seasoned marketing leader with twenty years of experience in Fortune 500 company Mondelez International, formerly Kraft Foods, Nabisco, and Cadbury. She is the founder of caringorganizer.com, a website offering inspiration, tips, and online meal schedulers to help people support others during difficult times, such as mourning a loved one or experiencing a serious illness.

Elisa holds an MBA and an MA in international affairs. She is recognized for building global and local brands and integrating corporate social responsibility into brand leadership.

Elisa's greatest passion is to cook for and nurture her family and friends. She always keeps homemade chicken soup on hand in case someone she knows could use an extra bit of comfort and support. She has dual Canadian and American citizenship and has lived in Canada, the US, Israel, and Singapore. Elisa currently lives in Morristown, New Jersey, with her husband, two teenage children, and lovable Newfie, Thomas.

Made in the USA
Monee, IL
18 November 2020

48354890R00121